World Class Politics:
Knoxville's 1982 World's Fair Redevelopment and The Political Process

Joe Dodd
University of Tennessee, Knoxville

Sheffield Publishing Company
Salem, Wisconsin

For information about this book, write or call:
Sheffield Publishing Company
P.O. Box 359
Salem, Wisconsin 53168
(414) 843-2281

Copyright © 1988 by Joe Dodd

ISBN 0-88133-356-5

Printed in the United States of America

For Dorothy

The research for these two studies and their preparation for publication involved contributions from many people. Regarding "Exposé" research, assistance was given graciously by city recorders Marsha Grandstaff and Cindy Abbott, who located taped records of key Knoxville City Council meetings. In addition, Richard Atkerson, Glen Hicks, and particularly Terry Haywood assisted in collecting and ordering material used in that project.

A very special note of thanks must go to Leon Ridenour who, as chairman of Citizens for a Better Knoxville, worked tirelessly for five years as my partner in the good fight. Special thanks also are extended to Councilwoman Bernice O'Connor whose dedication, determination, integrity, and courage could be the measure of the true public servant.

Research regarding "The World's Fair and After" was facilitated by help with financial data from city finance directors Rick Dulaney (1985) and Randy Vineyard (1987). Assistance in typing the manuscript was provided by Margaret Garrett, Sue Howerton, Irene Carney, Marie Horton, Debby Pierce, and Naina Pinkston. To all of these people, I extend my thanks.

I also am most grateful to Tom Ungs, professor of political science at the University of Tennessee, for again reading the entire manuscript with a critical eye and making a number of valuable comments, all of which were appreciated.

To my wife Dorothy goes my most heartfelt thanks and appreciation. Her observations, suggestions, patience, and support surely were crucial as this project moved from idea to completed manuscript. For so many reasons, this book is dedicated to her.

Joe Dodd
The University of Tennessee
Knoxville, Tennessee
August 1987

CONTENTS

Introduction

In a number of important respects, local governments in the United States are seriously lacking in their performance. Most readers would probably agree that a similar observation could be made about the United States government as well. In dealing with the politics of the 1982 World's Fair and its aftermath, the present study describes activities at both levels of government and in doing so identifies a number of core reasons for both political and administrative failures in our political system.

The United States can stand more world's fairs. What is questionable is whether we can safely continue to practice standard unbridled American politics with ever-increasing allocations of pork-barrel funds that strain our pocketbooks and fatten the wealthy while the nation's serious social and economic problems are ignored.

The general public desperately needs to know how its governments are working or not working. Meaningful reform must start with knowledge. This book provides real knowledge about actual political operations. I hope it will stimulate interest in working toward the reform of some of these operations.

The book is comprised of two separate studies conducted at different times dealing with the same set of political events surrounding Knoxville's 1982 World's Fair (Energy Expo '82, as it was called in its early years). The story begins in January 1977 and spans more than ten years to August 1987. In the middle is the World's Fair itself, which ran from May 1, 1982, to October 31, 1982.

The first study, presented here as Book One, was published privately and was first released in conjunction with the opening of the fair, although definitely not as a sanctioned publication of the fair. "Exposé," as the title suggests, is a hard hitting look behind the scenes at some five years of political activities by the Expo '82 promoters as they set about developing a support base for the international exposition.

Expo '82 was big; the stakes were high. As a result, the various participants played their roles with heightened intensity. The political aspects in numerous forms were accented and much more evident to an interested observer than one normally sees in politics.

This is no narrow, "downhome" study. The World's Fair political process was world class. The story ranges from Knoxville to Washington, from the elite to the masses, from electoral to administrative, from council to Congress, from the mayor's office to the Oval Office, from press release hype to reporter "spiked," from empirical fact to valued goal. It is a study of politics, lots of it, which goes to the heart of politics. Expo '82 is "one of the biggest political boondoggles I have ever seen," said U.S. Senator Ernest Hollings, who knew only a minor part of the story.

"Exposé" draws heavily on my experiences as a member of the opposition movement which initially attempted to obtain a popular vote on the exposition issue beginning in early 1977. When that failed, the movement continued (obviously with inadequate results) to offer public oversight about this private venture that was so heavily involved with the expenditure of large amounts of taxpayers' money. Where possible, my own experiences and notes have been buttressed by public records of specific events. I also have used newspaper accounts and other printed material extensively to supplement personal knowledge.

When "Exposé" was released in May 1982, it was very well received. As events unfolded over the following years, it has stood the test of time. But "Exposé" had sold out and new things were happening. Major events in the post-fair period included banks failing, millionaires going bankrupt, political power shattered, formerly powerful people jailed, fair buildings vacated, potential developers lost, politics surging up and then down in rapid succession. With each event and each passing year, colleagues, students, friends, and many citizens repeatedly asked when an "Exposé" update would occur.

In early 1987 Sheffield Publishing Company expressed an interest in seeing such a project undertaken. The time was ripe as we approached the fifth anniversary of the fair's opening. The story is not over. It may never be over. So much has happened that it is indeed time for a report on another five years of this remarkable political adventure.

Before setting out to make sense of those five years, however, a decision had to be made concerning how the new would be related to the old. The advice of friends, including those who had used the book in class, was unanimous. If you try to redo "Exposé," you'll surely lose something you don't want to lose. The feeling was that a

full scale reworking of the initial manuscript would lose
the mood, intensity, perspective, and "flow." Book Two,
"The World's Fair and After," thus emerged as a separate
entity, covering the fair itself and post-fair developments
up to August 1987.

Book I

Exposé: The Real Story Behind
The Knoxville World's Fair

Exposé was originally published in 1982. Except for editorial changes and a number of explanatory notes (in brackets), it remains as originally published.

INTRODUCTION, 1982

"The story behind its creation is a case history in political wheeling and dealing, a story that shows how the rich and influential can create a dream for themselves that may turn out to be a nightmare for the city and the state." So states the West Palm Beach *Post* in a major feature story on Knoxville's 1982 World's Fair.

And indeed, Knoxville International Energy Exposition (KIEE), or Expo '82, as it is more frequently called among Knoxvillians, does involve more than enticing promotional advertisements, spinning rides, fireworks, crowds, and endless lines. Behind the scenes lies a political process involving the manipulation of people, the exercise of power, and the expenditure of large amounts of public money.

Something called a world's fair, with the theme of energy, first raised its head in Knoxville in 1975. As legend has it around the Knoxville Chamber of Commerce building and the United American Bank Plaza, a concerned and creative citizen named Stewart Evans, executive director of the Downtown Knoxville Association, went to a meeting in Oklahoma, heard of the wonderful things that had come to Spokane, Washington, as a result of its Expo '74, came back to Knoxville with an idea, was either politely dismissed or ridiculed by everyone he talked to, but persevered, and ultimately convinced a few, then more, and finally all of the city fathers. Jake Butcher, chairman of United American Bank (the largest in the area), came forth, out of civic concern, as their leader, and together they overcame massive obstacles, climbed the bean stalk, slew the giant, and were on their way to creating a kingdom with super services, an expanded tax base, a united people, and worldwide recognition as the energy capital of the world. "It will provide an opportunity for fifty years of positive and progressive growth in a five-year span," stated a November 1976 Expo pamphlet.

A simpler version of the conception process exists. A paid lobbyist for a downtown interest group saw an opportunity to serve his clients. They saw big bucks, as did some key developers, architects, engineering consultants, suppliers, and bankers. Above all, a wealthy, brakeless banker named Jake Butcher saw a golden goose--with potential eggs for himself and those associated with him. The promoters followed the leader, exercised their political might, and brought home the goose. Get on board, stand aside, or get run over, went the motto.

The task of this book is not to produce a history of the 1982 World's Fair or a history of the Expo opposition movement, of which I was a prominent member. There is history; there is the movement. But the focus is both broader and narrower than the total Expo picture. It is broader in that the World's Fair story is a specific instance of American politics that says a great deal about the political process writ large. Related observations are made throughout the book, but the broader implication of Expo politics is the key subject of chapter 5. People like the Expo promoters don't just see opportunities. They make them. And they well know that to make opportunities in contemporary America, you need government influence and government money. The more the better. But what are the consequences for the broader public? For the truly needy?

The focus of the book is narrower than a total history of Energy Expo '82 in that it presents a concise image of four major public issues: the Expo sales job in Knoxville, the defeat of a referendum movement, the performance of the mass media, and the role and flow of money, the gravy, itself.

Chapter 1 explores the Expo sales job. What were the promises used in an attempt to sell Expo to Knoxville? What about performance? Obviously, all answers are not in regarding performance as this study goes to press in early 1982. But some are. At a public cost of over $21 million, the U.S. Pavilion was labeled the "showpiece" of the energy fair. [The cost of the building itself was $12.4 million.] In the post-fair period it was to become an energy research center.

In its January 1982 issue *Omni* magazine announced its list of "1981's Worst Scientific Achievements." The winner of its "Dim-Bulb Medal" is the World's Fair showpiece. It is not an energy-efficient building. But the laurels don't stop there. The General Accounting Office (GAO), the investigative arm of the U.S. Congress, recently called the pavilion a costly mistake. It has no established post-fair use. Performance? More follows.

There is a rumor abroad that the United States is an open, democratic society. Sometimes perhaps, but not in Knoxville--where public opinion polls from 1977 through

1979 showed an absolute majority against Expo, with an overwhelming majority in favor of a referendum. The second chapter deals with attempts over a three-year period to obtain a public vote on the issue. What happened? Why did some want a referendum? Why did others oppose it?

"Politics," some unknown wag observed, "follows the Golden Rule: He who has the gold makes the rules." This was no time for democracy in Knoxville, but it was a time for deception. And for hypocrisy: Mayor Randy Tyree had his minister pray over a city and a defeated opposition. A Knoxville attorney captures the essence: "This story probably isn't one you'd put in a small-town civics textbook."

The manipulation of people--as communist regimes know so well--is infinitely easier if the powers that be control the media. Chapter 3 turns to the media's role in Expo. The *Knoxville News-Sentinel*, the daily evening and Sunday morning paper, with a circulation of 101,000 and 158,000 respectively, is by far the larger of Knoxville's two newspapers. Fittingly located between the Knoxville Chamber of Commerce and United American Bank, the *News-Sentinel* in early 1982 was going into its sixth year as the major propaganda instrument of the Expo promoters, both on the editorial page and elsewhere.

The media story, however, is by no means all propaganda--even with the *News-Sentinel*. Indeed, on occasion the Knoxville media, and especially the *Knoxville Journal*, a morning daily with a circulation of 60,000, produced some excellent investigative reporting on Expo issues. But the accent is on "on occasion." When it counted, the flow of accurate information was overshadowed by the press release, by a timid and fawning journalism.

Chapter 4 turns to the issue of money and who gets it, which for the promoters always has been the heart and soul of the matter. "There is some misinformation going around," the official fair spokesman declared to a reporter in April 1981. "Not one single cent of municipal tax money is going for the fair site." The spokesman was lost in his own propaganda. In the city's case, he was in error by at least $33 million, plus interest.

Expo chairman Jake Butcher was powerful at home. "He's going to own Knoxville," *Newsweek* quotes City Councilwoman Bernice O'Connor. But there was more. Banker Butcher had a federal connection--in the form of President Jimmy Carter and his chief aide Bert Lance. These and other ties paid off.

Add up all the public money and the *known* public expenditures on the 65-acre Expo site and the total tops $80 million. And there were off-site opportunities for public "investments" as well.

A private $6.7 million parking garage was built. The privates put up $400,000, while the public threw in $6.3 million. And there was a renovated railroad station, again privately owned, with $4 million kicked in by John Q. Public. These are part of a $65 million, eight-project Expo development by close Butcher associates in which the taxpayers' toll is over $35 million (in federal and city money). For the public the risks seemed substantial. Suspicions of inflated costs abounded. No competitive bidding occurred, even on two publicly-owned buildings.

CHAPTER 1
Politics Is the Father of Lies

Sell It

Politicians and developers and their partners in public agencies are long on promises and short on performance.

Rare indeed is the occasion when one of these creatures has gone to bat for a vote or a buck or bureaucratic expansion without self-proclaimed service to the national interest, humankind, justice, peace in the world, or other such laudable goals. The answer lies in a particular project--a glittering project that all others would surely support if they only understood the way the boosters understood.

Equally as rare is the case where the actual achievements even remotely measure up to the assurances. But who would buy a project designed to serve narrow self-interest? And thus . . . the promoter must promote; the promoter must sell.

Know your target. Tailor the topic. Sell it.

The occasion was the monthly meeting of the Clean Environment Council (CEC) and the topic under discussion was Lower Second Creek, the proposed site of Energy Expo '82. The speaker back in March 1977 was John Ulmer, the executive director of Knoxville's Community Development Corporation (KCDC), a public agency responsible for both public housing and redevelopment in the city. Veteran *Knoxville News-Sentinel* reporter Carson Brewer, himself an environmentalist and nature lover and writer, captured the speaker's theme in his lead: "Restoration of Second Creek as a clean, attractive stream would be one of the benefits of Expo '82, according to one of the project's backers."

You have to know Knoxville's Second Creek to understand why Ulmer received a "friendly response" on this issue from an otherwise questioning CEC membership. Second Creek ran the length of the Expo site with some 1,200 feet in a tunnel and perhaps double that in a gully ranging up to 20 or so feet deep. It was dirty and clogged with trash, with little public access anywhere along its four-mile run through the city from Sharp Gap to the Tennessee River. Like so many other natural wonders of this Knoxville community, the creek through the years had been victimized by one wave of "progress" after another.

But now: "We would like to open it," proclaimed Ulmer, "give it back to the public," and "put some public open space down there."

A natural, unpolluted Second Creek was not the only promised benefit of the Expo promoters. There was something for everyone--a veritable blizzard of promises. To ask a question about one was to generate five more.

Was your inner-most soul wrapped up in a basketball arena for the University of Tennessee (UT)? Here was your chance, not just for an arena for the Big Orange, but, praise the Lord, for one larger than the University of Kentucky's Rupp Arena.

If not UT basketball, then perhaps your bag is UT academics. Expo would boost academic excellence . . . or at least produce more grant money for energy research.

Are you another kind of Knoxville booster? Expo would make Knoxville the undisputed energy research and development center, the "energy capital of the world," the "Cape Canaveral of Energy," Expo president S. H. ("Bo") Roberts, Jr., declared.

With Expo, the inner city would be resurrected: neighborhoods would be redeveloped, as would the business sector, with a doubling of retail sales in the downtown area. The city's tax base would be broadened. City employees would receive raises. Hospital facilities would be upgraded. Expo would solve Knoxville's pollution problem and its traffic problem.

And jobs. Would Expo ever create jobs! The more the promoters talked, the more the jobs appeared. The projected number started at less than 5,000, the bulk of which would be of a temporary, moonlighting variety, and rapidly increased to 10,800, of which 2,200 were permanent, and then on to 37,000, with 17,000 of them permanent. Finally--dare I say finally--with a burst of generosity for display on national T.V. in late 1981, Jake Butcher, chairman of the Expo board, "created" 3,000 more and raised the total number of new jobs to 40,000.

It was all there. An elevated "people mover" of some one and a half miles connecting the university, the Expo site, downtown, and the civic coliseum; perhaps rail service between Knoxville and Gatlinburg; perhaps even the re-establishment of contact with the national rail passenger service.

Does haphazard development bother you? Here was an opportunity not only for "fifty years of positive and progressive growth in a five-year span," but also "planned and orderly growth."

If you are worried about the future of mankind, or peace in the world, here is your opportunity to strike a blow. Join with us, said the promoters. We will bring the world together. Not only that. We will even bring Knoxville together.

There was something for everyone. Could there possibly be more? To know of The Promotion Saga is to know the answer. Of course, there was more. It would all be at no cost to the city. Indeed, Mayor Randy Tyree, always able to go one better, was boldly to proclaim that Expo would not even involve any risk for the city and its taxpayers. (When I first heard this claim, I thought of one of my father's favorite expressions: "I wouldn't believe that lie if I told it myself.")

The chamber-of-commerce type promotion made reference to everything but the kitchen sink . . . and making money. Some in the community were bold enough to raise the issue of money and money changers. There was a response.

In a pro-Expo letter to the editor, Oak Ridger Frank Callahan observed that he had "heard it said that businessmen are pushing Expo '82 to make money." His response to such audacious charges was quick and simple: "This is absurd." His reasoning was a bit tortuous, but interesting: "Businessmen are hard money people; they must make a profit." They could not possibly be "investing" in a "highly speculative venture" such as this. Therefore, they must be motivated by a "great civic spirit."

Surely it was just a coincidence that so many of the core supporters happened to be involved in appropriate economic activities: architectural firms, engineering firms, construction firms, building supply firms, tourist related services, and, of course, those who would handle the money, the bankers.

Utopia was at hand. No wonder chamber of commerce executive director Frank Deller, at a hearing on the Expo redevelopment plan in July 1977, was so enthusiastic as he declared: "Judgement Day is here." Surely Deller had no doubts as to how to pass muster. Vote the development plan, enter the promised land.

University of Tennessee history professor Richard Marius (since moved on to Harvard University) had earlier captured some of the flavor when he urged Knoxvillians to stand shoulder to shoulder and join in "singing that sweet invitational hymn":

Softly and Tenderly
Expo is calling,
Calling for you and me,
See in the papers
the benefits falling
Manna from Randy Tyree.

Knoxville! Knoxville!
Why are you doubting
So long?
Only believe in
Your Public Relations
And think not of what
Could go wrong.

Smile Like Rahab

But the ascension was not at hand in July 1977 . . .
or later. Some of the proclaimed glories were to appear, although the cause-effect relationships might not follow
those stated by the promoters. They were particularly
prone to claim credit for the interstate highway
improvements. A bottleneck at the corner of I-40 and I-75,
known not so affectionately as Malfunction Junction, was
to be eliminated. A semicircumferential I-640 was to be
built.

With the highway improvements the promoters had a
good thing going--almost the only thing for gaining
support among the general public. Thus, they were not inclined to note that land acquisition was already under way
well before Expo was a settled issue or that the governor
and state transportation officials stated that the changes
would occur, regardless of the fate of Expo.

There is little doubt that Expo did accelerate the
process of highway construction, but certain consequences
of the accelerated pace were ignored by the promoters.
Costs went from a 1977 projection of $55 million for a
completed system to an actual 1981 cost of $224 million
for an incomplete system with several temporary features,
especially around Malfunction Junction.

Some thought the costs were a bit exaggerated.
Others thought the system was poorly designed with I-640
coming back into I-40 well inside the city's high density
West Knoxville traffic. Still others observed that crash
construction leads not only to increased costs but also to
reduced quality and cited the washboard rhythm of I-640
to make the point.

Without question, however, the bulk of Knoxvillians supported the interstate improvements. They either felt their way around the traffic jams that accompanied massive construction, or they simply endured them.

There was also to be a partial truth to other promised benefits. Economic development did occur. One would hope so. Although the promoters early in their sales job foolishly tried to portray it otherwise, Knoxville was a boom-town well before Expo. It continued to boom. Because of Expo? Hardly. Without question the site itself changed (although to begin with it was far from the industrial slum area portrayed by the promoters). It would be difficult to spend over $80 million in public funds on less than 65 acres without creating changes. As to whether those changes fit the promises, that was another question.

Other things happened. Street beautification programs occurred in the immediate area of the site, as other city programs--schools, libraries, streets, parks-- outside the cherished downtown business sector languished in the throes of budgetary crisis and program cutbacks.

You can't concentrate resources without concentrating resources.

On the private side, cleanups did occur. (Just how much it would occur is still undetermined as this is being written in early 1982.) It would be surprising indeed if something didn't happen. Professor Marius surely wasn't totally off base when he observed that when strangers looked in on Knoxville, the unwashed fat lady would "pat her dirty hair in place and smile like Rahab welcoming Joshua's men."

Two Jackasses with Saddles

Other promises didn't stand up so well. The reader can speculate on whether the future of mankind or peace in the world is any more assured now than it was in 1977. Knoxvillians can also speculate on how successful the promoters have been in "bringing Knoxville together." Perhaps some indirect evidence is provided by University of Tennessee president Edward Boling, a self-proclaimed member of "the establishment."

"The disgruntled people aren't the people who count in this town," he reportedly told a *Wall Street Journal* reporter in December 1980. The observation is particularly interesting in view of the fact that opinion polls conducted in 1977, 1978, and 1979, at Boling's own university (but not, we can assume, with his encouragement) had revealed that an absolute majority of Knoxvillians opposed the exposition while an overwhelming majority of 84 percent favored a vote on the issue. In an attempt to obtain a referendum, Citizens for a Better Knoxville (CBK) had gathered the signatures of some 14,000 registered city voters.

Boling was right. The disgruntled people didn't count. No vote occurred. But not for lack of attempts.

Randy Schultz of the West Palm Beach *Post* quotes a Knoxville attorney in a May 1981 article: "This story probably isn't one you'd put in a small-town civics textbook."

Reasons for disenchantment were not restricted to the "masses." A Republican contractor, feeling blacklisted and cut out of the action by Expo chairman Jake Butcher and his friends and associates, was not speaking for himself alone when he observed to the *Wall Street Journal*: "Some people around here just have to operate under the pig theory."

Surely, large numbers would agree with Councilwoman Bernice O'Connor's position: "The taxpayers of Knoxville are being taken for a ride--it's pitiful." But exact percentages concerning opinions on this or other issues are not available. The UT College of Communications didn't conduct its yearly local-issues survey in either 1980 or 1981.

My own guess regarding public perceptions is that cynicism is up, politicians, developers, and bankers are down, and the chamber of commerce leadership of Knoxville is at least as unaccepted now as it was before Expo came on the scene.

It is doubtful if Expo has stimulated any increase in UT's supply of grant money; and even if it has, it doesn't seem to have positively affected academic programs. The UT administration in 1982, after five years of participating in the Expo promotional parade, seems to be more firmly tied to the city's business/banking community; but the resulting advantages for the university as a university are questionable.

The case is perhaps overstated. In an interview published in September 1980, UT's Boling, a member of the Expo Corporation board from the early days, observed: "The university can't wait. Our economists, business departments and engineers are so excited to learn new ways of energy conservation and also show what they know."

According to the chamber of commerce and other such organizations Knoxville remains the energy capitol of the world. Twenty miles west of Knoxville, Oak Ridge and its chamber, surely with more justification, say the same thing, as do, one might imagine, a lot of other cities and chambers. In fact, Oak Ridge puts up a sign at its city limits to advertise its energy leadership. In Knoxville, we don't have room for such things. Our city-limits signs advertise our political leadership: Mayor Randy Tyree--in script.

Air pollution also remains, except worse. Will it get better with Expo traffic and scattered, inadequate parking facilities? Like everywhere else, our traffic problem has been aided more by dramatic increases in Arab oil prices than anything else, including road improvements.

As for the promised "people-mover," mass-transit system, Bruce Ralston, a young UT geography professor, observed early in the game that it might turn out to be "two jackasses with saddles on them." Bruce was overly optimistic: no people mover exists, in any form. Nor is there any new rail service.

And the evidence increasingly mounts to demonstrate that the city is paying more for tax-base broadening than it is getting in new taxes. Those new jobs? The promoters' projected total of new permanent jobs was in excess of the total unemployment for all of the four-county Knoxville metropolitan area. But as employment data reveal, creating propaganda and creating jobs are two different things. The number of employed workers in Knox County for October 1981, the most recent data available at this writing, showed an absolute decline from the number of employed workers in September, while the unemployment rate rose from 6.5 percent to 7.1 percent.

Jobs? Of course jobs were created. How could you spend $80 million in public money without creating employment? But perhaps the promoters' initial figure of 5,000 new jobs, mostly of a temporary and moonlighting variety, was closer to the mark than any of their later creations.

Evidence indicates that neighborhood revitalization has fallen even further into the doldrums with Expo than before. As many of the surrounding residents feared, the promoters' meaning of "inner-city" revitalization was a rather narrow one. It simply meant the downtown business district, with the inner-city neighborhoods, not unlike all other parts of the city, feeling the effects of the concentration of resources on Expo and the downtown business area.

And what about Second Creek? On its way to "restoration" as a "clean attractive stream" Second Creek got waylaid. The 1,200 foot tunnel was extended another 1,300 feet, with 30 feet of fill. The promoters' natural way was to construct a four-acre, thirty-inch-deep ("Waters of the World") pond on top of the tunnel and fill. It is fitting to note that part of the cost of this project was covered by U.S. Department of the Interior "heritage and conservation" funds. But even with planned development some things can go wrong, can't they?

Unlike Atlanta

And did we have assurances on planning! Planning, or at least talk of it, was in. From the beginning of The Promotion Saga in early 1977 the mayor had pointed out the advantages of such a thing. Expo chairman Jake Butcher noted that Expo would give Knoxville planned development, unlike the situation in Atlanta. With both the mayor and "the man" proclaiming, surely we were on our way to demonstrate how to really plan.

Four years later, construction on the site was proceeding rapidly. The city administration was constructing an exhibition center and office building complex. Planning had been so thorough that the city had "forgotten" to conduct a feasibility study regarding the two facilities--as to their locations, their sizes, their uses, or their compatibility with other city facilities. In his haste, the mayor also "forgot" the concept of competitive bidding.

Some critics had the audacity to ask: "What do we do with these facilities after Expo?" Alex Harkness, the presumed developer at the time, was quick with an answer: Use them "for whatever the city wants to use them for."

It was not just a question of no contact with the general public. The commitment to the project by the mayor was signed, sealed, and delivered before the city had discussed the issue with the Tourist Commission or its administrative arm, Knoxvisit, the groups most directly concerned with the issue of conventions and convention facilities.

In November 1980 one tourist commissioner reportedly said in regard to the exhibition hall: "We've been sold a bill of goods down there." Oddly enough, the commissioner was William Fortune, president of Rentenbach Engineering, a major booster of Expo, a former board member of the Expo Corporation, and, with his firm serving as the Expo construction manager, a major recipient of Expo largess. Even so, he was uncertain as to why the building should be a convention center. The mayor just began "calling it that and tried to get the people behind it." With the city locked into a $1.9 million a year payment, "our money will be tied up and we can't get a decent convention center anywhere else."

(Some time later, when the exhibition building was already under way, it occurred to someone that exhibition halls had exhibitions and that some form of access was needed to get major exhibits into the building.)

The mini-wave of protest over the exhibition hall, not unlike the few other public complaints that came from among elite elements, passed quickly. Aside from a few remote voices crying in the jungle of greed, not even a ripple formed regarding the far more absurd city-financed office building, even though the city government had no known need or use for the building. Indeed, the city at the time was still in the process of moving into the new $33 million City-County Building.

But it was not only the exhibition hall and office building complex that has passed the "unlike Atlanta" planning test so well. With over five years of presumed planning behind the Expo project, *News-Sentinel* reporter Bob Hetherington wrote a story in February 1981 on planning for post-Expo use of the site. His opening line: "It is still a guess what will happen to the once-blighted Lower Second Creek Valley after the World's Fair." But the planners were at work, trying to deal with a largely locked-in situation. The reporter observed that they had identified "some" of the issues.

"What happens to the [Southern] Railroad track running through the site?" Getting rid of the railroad was one of the great benefits which Expo was to bring. Car storage facilities were absorbed into the site but some three-fourths of a mile of Southern track, running the length of the elongated site, was left in place, a result of the prohibitive cost of replacing the bridge over the Tennessee River. What happens after Expo? The posed question was answered by A. J. ("Flash") Gray, a retired Tennessee Valley Authority (TVA) planner who is heading the planning team: "It just isn't feasible in the foreseeable future to get the railroad track out of there."

"How will residents get into and around the valley?" Gray was perceptive: "Of prime importance [in the post-Expo period] is getting people into the site" so that they can reach the park, the lake, and the amphitheater. A minor problem arose when it was discovered that all three public facilities were surrounded by private property. And there was that problem of getting large exhibitions into the exhibition hall. Many in the Fort Sanders residential area to the west of the site thought that the "planned" redevelopment would not increase traffic through their neighborhood. Sometimes foresight is no sight. Core access to the site will be from the west via Fort Sanders. [Interestingly enough, as of mid-1987 the core access issue remains in limbo, with plans still being worked out.]

"What is the demand for downtown housing?" A related question that wasn't asked: If a demand exists, will private developers allow the Expo site to be the location for meeting such demands or will they try to play their own game, developing the areas that they want to develop rather than the one on a steep slope overlooking the Southern line to Alcoa?

"Will Knoxvillians use a downtown park?" A good question, especially since the city had already spent $1 million to acquire the 9.2 flood-zone acres and would have to spend substantially more in turning it into a park after Expo. It's also a good question, given the physical condition of other public facilities in the city. The Tyson Park restrooms illustrate the city's approach. Use a federal grant to build a facility, let it clean itself for several years, padlock it a few years after health conditions demand that something be done, and apply for a federal grant to replace the dilapidated facility. As one might guess, this is perhaps an exaggeration . . . but only slightly so. I'm not sure if the restrooms were built with federal money. [My hyperbole returns to earth. In 1985 the city used federal grant money to clean up Tyson Park. Under new Mayor Kyle (Tennis Court) Testerman (1983-), the bulk of the money went toward Omni Court reconstruction of the tennis courts, but the restrooms were restored. Maintenance under Testerman has led to speculation that the circle will be broken.]

"Who is responsible for the $3 million amphitheater and how will it be used?" As the state languished near rock bottom in state funding for its educational system, as the prisons bulged at the seams, let's all join in the cheer: "It's only $3 million." And indeed, it's true. The $3 million, plus another million for the state's program at the facility, plus perhaps a million or two in cost overruns, is minor in comparison with the promoters' designed $20 million-plus state-financed arena, which no doubt would have experienced at least $5 million in cost overruns.

(Postscript 1982. The writer was premature. As the exposition came closer and closer Governor Lamar Alexander climbed higher and higher on the bandwagon. With the announcement of additional money for various purposes in December 1981, he noted that the state's Expo contribution was now $10 million. No such announcements were made for the state's educational system.)

Boondoggle

If the above issues could raise a few eyebrows about the thoroughness of the planning process, another one could blow the top off. For over four years, the federal pavilion--the showpiece of the 1982 World's Fair--was going to be a high-powered energy research center in the post-Expo period. Oh, the superlatives this wondrous thing called forth! The bubble burst about a year before the exposition was to open.

The U.S. Department of Energy (DOE) had rejected the building well over a year earlier. DOE already had more empty buildings in the neighboring city of Oak Ridge than it could handle. The U.S. General Services Administration (GSA), the federal agency which handles office space for the U.S. government, didn't want it. TVA didn't want it. And then, with this $12.4 million white elephant already under construction the University of Tennessee administration, after providing four years of we-want-it legitimacy to the project, was finally pressured by the *Knoxville Journal* and state Senator Victor Ashe into making an announcement. UT would not be able to use the facility because conversion costs would be too high.

Significantly, only two months earlier UT's expressed "interest" in post-Expo usage of the pavilion had enabled the promoters to thwart an effort in the U.S. Senate to turn the pavilion into a less-costly temporary structure. The UT administration did its job well--for the promoters. As for the taxpayers. . . .

In a March 1981 report the General Accounting Office (GAO), the investigative arm of Congress, called the pavilion a "costly" mistake because the Department of Commerce, the reigning federal agency for Expo, had no plans for post-Expo use and was nevertheless building a permanent facility, contrary to GAO's "prior recommendation" calling for temporary construction under such circumstances.

The GAO report further noted that a Commerce official explained that the Department had gone with the permanent facility because "considerable pressure" had been exerted by the promoters. Why the pressure? The promoters needed the permanent facility as a lever to obtain private and public financing for other aspects of the fair. Beautiful!

Perhaps we now know why Senator Ernest Hollings of South Carolina referred to Expo as "one of the biggest political boondoggles" he had ever seen. Such a statement by Hollings is significant. Unlike most members of Congress he still knew a boondoggle when he saw one.

For the bulk of his colleagues, the back-slapping, pork-barrel trade-offs are so much a part of their very political beings and make-believe world that the funding of a federal office building in Milwaukee at twice the normal cost was just routine and expected. It was the solution to Milwaukee center city redevelopment and absolutely essential for the national interest of the United States, if, of course, Wisconsin congressmen would only recognize that the Tennessee-Tombigbee Waterway was the solution to economic revitalization in Alabama and Tennessee, and also absolutely essential for the national interest of the United States.

To read through the annual public works appropriation is to see politics at its best, or its worst, depending on your perspective. The bulk of what is done is "public" only in a narrow sense and "works" only for a select few. It is compatible with the national interest only if the national interest is defined as boosting bureaucratic expansionism, furthering the reelection imperative of congressmen, and stuffing the pockets of a few.

But the public works syndrome does not stop with the public works appropriation. It penetrates every department of the U.S. government. And thus we find the U.S. Travel Service in the Department of Commerce doing its thing with the international exposition: maintaining (perhaps even expanding) itself, providing goodies to help out the reelection prospects of Senators Sasser and Baker and others in the Tennessee delegation, while at the same time providing a little more stimulus for the already booming Knoxville economy.

In a very real sense, then, the federal pavilion is a showpiece, a monument. It is a monument to the reality of American pork-barrel politics. It is also a monument to the reality of the U.S. energy problem.

In regard to Expo, Senator Lowell Weicker observed that we needed "energy solutions" not an "energy carnival." Senator Hollings asked: why should we "expose our failures" to the world?

Undaunted by such observations, the Expo promoters forged on. One Expo official approvingly observed: the fair will "be a United States forum for delivering an energy message to the world." He was right, but he was coming from the wrong direction.

The U.S. Pavilion, GAO concluded, is an energy failure. It was not designed to be an energy-efficient building. The Department of Energy caught the paradox and thought others would also: given the energy theme of the exposition, this "showpiece" of the Knoxville International Energy Exposition "could be a significant embarrassment to the United States."

So Much For Planning

Perhaps chairman Butcher was right in observing that Knoxville's planning was to be "unlike Atlanta." Some would argue that the Knoxville group had a distinctively Knoxvillian approach.

Back in June 1977, Professor Marius was having a bit of fun lamenting some of the past "planning" glories of Knoxville. But now, he observed, "our businessmen and their flunkies on the evening paper and in the city administration are telling us that all this will change with Expo. Expo is thus a great conversion experience, and these people who have lived all their lives in civic vulgarity have now been born again in a great outpouring of taste. They have changed their ways and do us good."

Marius was premature. Knoxville's "new" planning looks like propaganda plus the same old K-town principle: after economic greed and political expediency comes coping. (Coping as in cope, that is, in its technical "use." Coping is one of the many creative words produced by the bureaucrats. Roughly translated it means: How the hell can I get out of this mess?)

In fact the only real plan for the Lower Second Creek valley that was set forth in a meaningful time frame (that is, before it was too late to plan) was undertaken by something called the RUDAT team well before any construction activity on the site began.

The Regional Urban Design Assistance Team is a program of the American Institute of Architects (AIA). At the request of a local community, AIA puts together a team of outside professional architects, engineers, urban planners, and economists who go into the community for an intensive five days of study, culminating with a recommended plan of action for the community.

In the Knoxville case arrangements were made by the local AIA chapter and the Metropolitan Planning Commission (MPC), the public planning body of the City of Knoxville and Knox County, for such a team to study and make recommendations for use of the valley after the exposition.

The team was all set for a visit in March 1978, but the Expo promoters apparently thought too much criticism would flow their way from the various neighborhood groups that were scheduled to meet with the RUDAT team. As a result, MPC executive director George Siler (soon to become an executive vice president with the Expo Corporation) abruptly postponed the session at the last minute, presumably at the insistence of the promoters.

The postponement led Annette Anderson, the local director of the RUDAT project, to submit a letter of resignation. Said Anderson: "I am disappointed that as a community, we are unable to examine major public issues in an open participatory way."

Ultimately, the promoters, presumably feeling that they were in better control of the situation, convened the gathering a year later in March 1979.

This is not the place for a full report of the RUDAT recommendations. Suffice it to say that the team was thinking right. It was serious about energy. Fill the valley with a development that will serve as a demonstration of energy conservation. The team was serious about total urban redevelopment. In this potentially beautiful setting along the banks of a revitalized Second Creek, build a model "town-in-town," quality residential area, accompanied by needed commercial services, that would begin the process of bringing people back into the old center city. Above all, coordinate the development of the exposition with the post-Expo redevelopment of the site.

Publicly, the team's report was greeted with enthusiasm by the political and economic elite of Knoxville. Privately, the report went the way of Second Creek. It was covered up with thirty feet of dirt. So much for energy, redevelopment, planning.

No Cost, No Risk

With benefits disappearing like integrity in public life, one might assume that costs would go down. Of course, it would be hard to drop below no cost and no risk. But since changes were occurring in benefits, something must be occurring in cost. As illogical as it may seem, since logic says that costs can't go down, they must go up. Logic (or illogic) notwithstanding, costs have gone up.

As of writing time in early 1982 the total *direct, on-site* public costs--at the federal, state, and local levels--had outstripped $80 million, with the promoters still striving for more. The city had led the way. It had initially put in $11.66 million which, combined with Expo '82 funds, was supposed to handle land acquisition, relocation, and site improvements. Supposedly no risk was involved. Resale of the land, the mayor and other promoters said repeatedly, will cover all city cost.

Fortunately for the critic, four acres of the most valuable of the publicly acquired land (the total having been reduced from 80 acres to some 30 acres because of dramatic cost overruns) was resold earlier than expected as a result of the Station '82 developments, thus enabling rough analysis of total resale possibilities. The best guess is a $6 million loss, plus interest. [No additional land had been sold as of mid-1987, and the city was still absorbing all of its "no-risk investment."]

The city's $11.66 million wasn't enough. In the eight-project Station '82 package were a city-backed exhibition hall and an office building--both to be used by Expo during the exposition. In a highly complex financial arrangement the city obligated itself to a yearly payment of at least $1.9 million over a 30 year period, the equivalent cost of retiring a $21 million bond issue at 10 percent.

Mayor Tyree at first assured and reassured--no cost, no risk. Then Bill Ricker, city operations officer, was forced to admit under oath in a court case to a city-calculated yearly loss of $360,000. This was a best-of-all-possible-worlds figure. More likely there will be a loss of something on the order of $900,000 a year over 30 years. [From the perspective of 1987, even my estimate was overly optimistic. Although difficult to calculate, the loss at a minimum is running at least half-again higher than my 1982 estimate.]

There were other "incidental" on-site expenses for the city. The mayor committed the city to a pavilion. (Something had to be done to get pavilion-space announcements off dead center.) How much the city will end up paying for the pavilion is still up in the air. The mayor also committed $750,000 to replace the front of a private parking garage. As it turned out, he illegally took the money out of a bond issue intended for other purposes.

In addition, the city is the proud owner of a $250,000 pedestrian bridge across Second Creek. With 2,500 feet of Second Creek in a tunnel, one might assume that a path could have been found without building a bridge a short distance above the beginning of the tunnel. No way. This is a bridge we can all be proud of. And it is absolutely essential--in the national interest, so to speak.

The above city costs involved on-site activities. Other city costs, of course, were incurred for off-site projects designed to beautify the downtown area. And there were millions of dollars associated with the additional services for the visitors. Still other millions were used to subsidize private development projects in the downtown area.

These costs, not unlike the on-site ones, seemed like rather obvious costs. And the risks associated with several of the projects seemed like rather obvious risks. But it just doesn't matter. The promoters, including the mayor and other political figures, remained undaunted. Their answer was simple. No cost. No risk.

Birds Sing, Hogs Wallow

There is not much debate over how promoters and politicians are able to become so adept at handling promises, deception, half truths, and lies. Practice makes perfect, as the saying goes.

But debate sometimes rages on over why politicians and those who manipulate them engage in such practices. Perhaps the best explanation is what a social scientist might call a "functional" explanation. Deception is there because it works. Politicians and those who steer politicians use promises, use deceit, use the language to achieve their real purposes. And they are frequently successful because too few are aware of what is happening.

And thus the end brings us back to the beginning. "Politics is the father of lies," so states a recent book by political scientists John Donovan, Richard Morgan, and Christian Potholm *(People, Power, and Politics)*. In politics language is not necessarily used to inform, to clarify, to educate. Instead it may be, and indeed frequently is, used to deceive, to confuse, to promote, with truth being at best irrelevant, at worst, an obstacle to overcome.

The above remarks do not mean that the techniques of deception are automatically successful. In some instances members of the general public may not simply accept a questionable bill of goods. (They may not be able to stop what is happening, but they nevertheless may know what is happening.)

Surely in the Knoxville case the promoters didn't seem overly confident that they could easily sell the general public on the Expo issue. They hedged their bet by getting City Council to take initial action on a bond issue of $11.66 million before an attempt was made to sell the project to the local people. Then when the sales job sputtered, almost stalled, they pulled out all the stops in their effort to kill a popular vote on the issue.

CHAPTER 2
A Bad Time for Democracy

A Real Peoplestate?

"Stockholm, March 23--Sweden voted today to support limited expansion of nuclear energy." So stated the *New York Times* lead on its coverage of the 1980 vote that had been cast by 75 percent of Swedish voters after a heated campaign.

Swedish Prime Minister Thorbjorn Falldin had backed the antinuclear option. He had lost. The pronuclear options had received over 58 percent of the vote. But legally, the vote was not binding. What did his conscience dictate? "My conscience," Falldin said, "is not the decisive factor. A large number of people have stated their frame of mind. And that is the decisive factor."

And thus, on a major, extremely controversial public issue, the country *(Keesing's Contemporary Archives* tells us) with by far the largest per capita production of nuclear powered electricity, had acted decisively--and democratically.

Five months before the Swedes went to the polls, an election had occurred in Knoxville, Tennessee. The results were in. "A referendum for Expo '82 has been held, and it won," the *Knoxville News-Sentinel* boldly proclaimed in its post-election editorial of October 14, 1979.

Was this again an illustration of democracy at work? To the contrary. Indeed, some would recall the *Sentinel's* past three years of opposition to a referendum and see in its latest hoax just one small fragment of a larger episode that indicated not the expression, but rather the perversion of democracy.

That was my feeling as I formulated a letter to the editor in response to his interpretation of the mayoral election. Was a vote for incumbent Mayor Randy Tyree a vote for Expo? Or was this more *News-Sentinel* hypocrisy? My choice was the latter.

Tyree's two chief opponents did not run anti-Expo campaigns. Both argued that they would be more effective in implementing Expo than Tyree. As for Tyree, he treated Expo like the plague. In his many advertisements, he never once claimed credit for Expo; and in the single ad in which Expo is even mentioned, he is quoted as saying that the real issue is "not Expo: I didn't start Expo, it was on my desk when I became your mayor." Tyree's goal most explicitly was to muffle the whole Expo question.

As I pointed out in my letter, the *Sentinel's* news and editorial role in the election, along with the editor's refusal to print a pre-election letter from me (and one from Citizens for a Better Knoxville chairman Leon Ridenour, and perhaps others as well) in which Tyree's role in the exposition was raised, clearly indicated that the *Sentinel* editor, like Tyree, did not want Expo to be the issue or even an issue. (I did not add that CBK, the key pro-referendum, anti-Expo organization in the city, did not see fit to endorse any candidate in the election.)

I concluded by observing that, in spite of a *News-Sentinel* editorial encouraging participation in the election so that we might "Have a Real Peoplestate" and ideal weather conditions, only 32 percent of the registered voters went to the polls. Our mayor received 9,000 fewer votes than he had obtained four years earlier and remained in office with the expressed support of 17 percent of the registered voters.

Some referendum. Some victory. Some "Peoplestate."

As strange as it might seem, on the question of Expo as an issue in the campaign, I had company from none other than Tyree himself. Perhaps it was the flush of victory. Perhaps it was a touch of integrity. Be that as it may. When questioned by a reporter, Tyree responded that the issue was not Expo.

Such straightforward responses from Tyree on Expo, however, were few and far between, as had been patently obvious during the previous three years when the Expo opposition was trying to obtain a real referendum.

A Movement Was Born

The referendum issue first raised its head on January 11, 1977, on the occasion of the passage by Knoxville City Council of an initial resolution for an $11.66 million Expo bond issue. Some in attendance at the council meeting stepped up, arguing that a program as important as the one proposed should be decided by a popular vote.

Others, including Councilwomen Bernice O'Connor and Willie Hembree, stated that too little was known about the program. Mrs. Hembree observed that although numerous copies of the draft environmental impact statement on the project were in Knoxville, the promoters had not provided copies to council members.

Mrs. O'Connor's motion for a two-weeks delay in order to study a massive project that was to occur more than five years hence was unacceptable to the promoters and was defeated by a 6-3 vote, with the bond issue then passing by a 5-2 vote. It was a portent of things to come.

While Bernice was saying the promoters had bypassed the people with a "blitz," and the promoters were beginning the process of changing the world, I sat at home, perhaps reading about American politics. Like essentially all of Knoxville's population, I knew nothing about a forthcoming bond resolution.

The *News-Sentinel* had carried a front page Expo story on the day of the council session. It talked about the wonderful things that Expo would bring to Knoxville and Knoxvillians, all of which had been neatly presented by the promoters the night before at a reception for city officials. Buried in the story on the "jump" (inside) page was a reference to the bond issue, scheduled for a vote that night.

Several months after I had become involved in the Expo business, Nancy Sharp, a student who had interviewed me on the Expo issue, presented me with a copy of a term paper she had written on the referendum issue for another professor. She started her paper with a quote from Floyd Hunter's *Community Power Structure,* a classic study in the field: "It has been evident to the writer for some years," Hunter wrote, "that policies on vital matters affecting community life seem to appear suddenly. They are acted upon, but with no precise knowledge on the part of the majority of citizens as to how these policies originated or by whom they are really sponsored."

So it was in Knoxville. Crucial elements of the Knoxville power structure had been at work for some time. They had now beaten off a movement for a deferral. They had gotten by city council on a bond issue. But they were not home free. They would have to contend with elements of the "masses" for almost three years. The issue in contention was a referendum, a vote by the people, on the Expo issue.

City council's reaction to Mrs. O'Connor's request for a two-week delay had made it abundantly clear that obtaining a referendum from council would be a most difficult task. Nevertheless, a number of people in the city thought that the exposition offered substantial risks for Knoxville. A referendum movement was born.

The present study is not designed to present details concerning the evolution of this movement. It is sufficient to indicate that the movement in its early form was largely ineffective in its key tasks, the formation of a petition and the gathering of signatures on that petition. Because of the existence of chaotic leadership conditions a new organization, Citizens for a Better Knoxville, was formed. Ultimately CBK, a group of political neophytes who came together because the job wasn't being done by anyone else, became the core organized effort for a referendum and against the exposition. In this reluctantly formed group, I reluctantly emerged as a spokesman and researcher.

CBK, Councilwomen Bernice O'Connor and Willie Hembree, some of the inner-city neighborhood organizations, and a few other "leaders" provided the pressure for referenda by articulating the issues, speaking for what ultimately was determined to be well over a majority of Knoxvillians, and obtaining through the formal action of Mrs. O'Connor and Mrs. Hembree in 1977 and later by Bernice alone, five city council votes on the referendum issue. Each of these efforts failed to overcome the political power of the Expo Corporation and its allies in city government. A final effort for a referendum dealt not with the existence of the exposition itself, but with an attempt to restrict the amount of city money used in the project. It too failed.

Delay It

Immediately after the promoters' initial victory at the January 1977 city council meeting they turned their sales job on the public. Council had been overcome. Now the public had to be handled. That task was not to be easy. In fact, S. H. Roberts, Jr., the president of the Expo Corporation, later said that he had not anticipated as much in the way of negative reaction.

Pressure from the opposition was strong, and it was having some success. A large percentage of the Knoxville population clearly was in favor of a referendum. By late March Councilwomen Hembree and O'Connor thought the time was ripe for city council action on the referendum issue. They presented the motion at the council meeting on April 5, 1977.

A few days earlier, on April Fool's Day, Bernice had stated: "I don't believe a single councilman will vote against it." Wasn't it obvious what the people wanted? Wasn't it the democratic way?

Indeed, things did look bad for the promoters. The masses were surging. The promoters saw it in their propaganda meetings. They saw it in letters to the editor. And no doubt they ran into it on the street as well as on the cocktail circuit.

The promoters had their solid majority on council; but even in a manipulative political system, the vote does occur. The promoters and their supporters on council were on the hot seat.

When powerful people run into problems with the masses in a "democracy," they turn to a frequently used political strategy--the delay. And so it was with Bernice's motion for a referendum. It was waylaid by a substitute motion calling for deferral. The substitute motion passed by a 5-4 vote with the mayor breaking a 4-4 Council tie. (Councilwoman Jean Teague, up for re-election in the fall, was absent. No explanation for her unusual absence was offered.)

Led by the mayor, the Expo supporters on council had raised the appropriate "delaying" questions. Why should we schedule a referendum on Expo before the U.S. Commerce Department in Washington approves it, or before the Bureau of International Expositions (BIE) in Paris (the international organization that sanctions such events) approves it? Both of these bodies would act before April 27. If they don't approve, no exposition would occur and the issue of a referendum would be moot. All along, of course, the questioners knew that approval in Washington and Paris was automatic--if no referendum was scheduled.

The council majority handled the delay strategy perfectly. *Knoxville Journal* reporter Larry Aldridge reported (correctly) that, "despite the close vote, none of the councilmen expressed opposition to a referendum." Indeed, Councilman M. T. Bellah said emphatically: "I want a referendum, but I want it deferred until after April 1977."

Mike Cavender of the *News-Sentinel* was not quite so correct. He gave the voting majority an editorial boost by accepting their expressed line as reality. "At issue last night was not whether a referendum should be held, but whether one should be officially approved before the BIE announces its decision on the matter. . . ." In reality, the issue was precisely what Cavender said it was not. Indeed, had Cavender checked the record he would have known that all five of the deferral votes were from people-- Bellah, Jack Sharp, Rex Davis, Theotis Robinson, and Tyree--who had earlier opposed a two-week deferral in January.

The strategy worked. The majority didn't have to vote no on a referendum and risk alienating a public that included potential voters. Bernice and Willie had been sandbagged--by an avalanche of feather pillows.

April 27 came and went, and, sure enough, Expo passed muster in Washington and Paris. But things still were not going well in Knoxville, even after months of promotional work by the Expo people and largely favorable coverage by the media.

Two days after Paris, professor Jack Haskins, director of the University of Tennessee's Communications Research Center, released the results of a public opinion poll. It showed 53.5 percent of registered city voters against Expo, 31 percent in favor, with 15.5 percent undecided. Even more astounding were the opinions expressed regarding the referendum question.

A referendum was favored by 84 percent of the "completely representative sample," as Haskins described it. CBK's experience confirmed the overwhelming support for a referendum. To ask for a signature on the referendum petition was to get it.

The information was there; the public support was there. It was time for another push for a referendum.

Things were complicated by Councilwoman Bernice O'Connor's back surgery, but she had announced her intentions in mid-April and her referendum resolution was on the agenda for May 17. Bernice was out of her sickbed and to the council meeting. But for every challenge, there is a response. Councilman "Smiley" Blanchard said he was sick, couldn't attend the meeting, and wanted a deferral.

Bernice was obviously trying to stay low key. But she was furious. The accepted procedure for a council member requesting a delay is to contact the member who put the item on the agenda beforehand. This resolution had been up for four weeks. Blanchard had not contacted her.

"I'm sick and tired of the delays and pressures. It's time for council to act," Bernice boomed out. A roar of approval thundered back from the "hundreds of residents" that packed the assembly hall. It had the impact of a paper tiger.

The promoters had spoken quietly before the meeting. They knew that something had to be done. They had the necessary support on city council, but those supporters were restless. How could a council member oppose a vote by the people and not risk defeat in the next election? The promoters had an answer. They offered a change in financing, another reason for delay. The state legislature, they said, had just passed legislation that might allow the exposition to go forth without the city's bond issue.

It was the fig leaf Councilman Theotis Robinson needed. He called for a council workshop so the issue could be studied closely. His substitute motion to defer to a workshop was supported by five other council members, four of whom insisted that they were just voting for the delay, that they supported a referendum.

The pillows had fallen again. Without specifically voting against a referendum, the council majority had managed to skirt around the referendum issue once more.

Bernice verbally fought back. She called Robinson's reasoning "a red herring." "They didn't get to me, but I believe they got to the rest of 'em over the weekend." She had the support of the indignant and intractable crowd. Tyree was forced to call a recess when he could not shut off the comments and complaints from the audience.

The referendum forces didn't know it at the time, but it was their finest hour. Bernice had performed well in her formal position. The points had been made from the floor. But most importantly, the crowd had turned out, even more than in April, and it had let the public officials know its position, loudly, with no uncertainty. Bernice could perform again; speakers could perform again; but the crowd could not be held. Too many were too cynical. We were to feel the impact two weeks later at the council meeting on May 31.

The Canary and the Preacher

The workshop was held. A new finance plan was presented by the promoters. The risk for the city taxpayers is removed, said the mayor, said Expo president S. H. Roberts, Jr., said other promoters. The city's redevelopment agency, KCDC, would sell over $40 million in private bonds, with repayment dependent on the success of the exposition and the redevelopment of the site after the exposition. The plan is a "gimmick," CBK spokesmen responded.

Now the promoters needed to have city council pass a resolution calling for a formal public hearing, as required under state law, for the purpose of establishing the proposed exposition site as a redevelopment area with interim use for the exposition. But the promoters didn't put the item on the agenda for the May 31 meeting. Instead, they would bring it in the back door and in the process sidestep another referendum move.

Bernice had her referendum resolution on the agenda again. This time she was ready. She was determined to force council to vote a referendum up or down. She and Willie had it worked out. Willie would move for a referendum. Bernice expected the promoter councilmen to offer a substitute motion to approve the establishment of a public hearing on the redevelopment project. Bernice would come back with another substitute motion which differently stated would get back to the referendum. That would be it. *Robert's Rules of Order* allowed no more substitutions.

Everything went according to the script--up to a point. Willie offered her motion, the promoters' council supporters offered a substitute motion; Bernice jumped in with her substitute motion. Then something was added. Theotis Robinson probably didn't know what to do, so he did the only thing he could. He moved to table Bernice's motion. Bernice knew her parliamentary procedures, and she shot back. If the substitute is tabled, the whole set of motions is tabled, including the motion regarding the public hearing. City law director John Roach ruled against Bernice. She requested an opinion from city council's attorney, Harold Mills. Mills said he thought Mrs. O'Connor was right. He looked it up, found it, and read it out. Bernice was right. She thought she had them. She would get her vote on a referendum. Bernice was wrong.

The mayor, with much verbiage, said that council really didn't have any established rules. Nowhere was it spelled out that *Robert's Rules of Order* prevailed, he said. Bernice responded: "The law director has looked at his *Robert's Rules of Order* ever since I've been on this council." Mayor Tyree had an answer.

"This is like that riddle," the mayor said. "Where does a 300-pound canary sit? The answer is: anywhere it wants." Like that canary, the mayor ruled, council can use just about any rules it wants. And thus, parliamentary procedure went under the table, the table was approved by a 7-2 vote, and the motion for the redevelopment hearing was passed by the same margin.

"You all have rammed this down our throats tonight," said Councilwoman Bernice O'Connor.

Political power had been exercised, with a flippant disregard for parliamentary procedure. For the third time, the promoters had worked their will--not only to thwart a popular vote on the Expo issue, but also, and far more important, to do so in a manner consciously designed to cloud the responsibility of those who had voted against the views of an overwhelming majority of Knoxvillians.

Now the promoters' floor leader, Mayor Tyree, tried to sanctify it all with the Word--from the minister of his own church, the most prestigious of the Methodist churches in the area.

As the noise of the crowd started to subside, the mayor spoke: "If I might add one comment. . . . I'm afraid unfortunately that our community is going to become somewhat divided, over the issue of Expo '82. I don't know how anybody else feels about it, but Dr. Toombs Kay is in the audience tonight. He is the pastor of Church Street United Methodist Church. And if there is one thing that each and every individual in this city should do, it's [pause] to have a little prayer about the kinds of decisions that we are going to make. . . . And if it's not an imposition on Dr. Kay, I'd ask him to come forward at this time for a brief prayer."

Kay was near the front of the hall, waiting. He moved to the podium.

"Mr. Mayor, I am pleased to do this, because I think as we speak of an energy exposition in Knoxville, whatever is decided, that the greatest need of this great city is to have the energy of the spirit of God in its people.

"Let us pray."

The words came forth--in resonant voice, smooth flowing, with appropriate pauses, and unity of themes.

"Lord God, we thank You for Knoxville. This is our town. There are many things about it that we love, and cherish [pause] and defend. There is [sic] some things we want to change. And we pray that You will work with us, in our lives [pause] in our minds and hearts [pause] to labor as individuals and as groups, using those processes that are given to us, to make the decisions that can send our community into the future--a better place to live and work, and grow, and thrive. Empower these who are in positions of decision-making authority. And give them [pause] the right, of course [pause] to disagree, but never to be [pause] totally [pause] disagreeable. And grant to all of us that we may seek the best, and the finest, and the noblest, and speak through us to the great issues that are before us as we beg this, Oh God. Wanting to be Your people, standing in need of Your grace.

"Amen and Amen."

"Mr. Mayor, Mr. Mayor, could I say just a word, please?" said the brusque, urgent voice of the burly man who reached the podium almost before Kay's slim figure had moved back.

The unidentified man, I later discovered, was Guy Milam, pastor of a small North Knoxville Baptist Church. He groped for words, spoke haltingly, but amid the starts and stops, the intensity, came the message.

"I am appalled tonight. . . . Very frankly, honestly, there is nobody in this world who believes in prayer any more than I do. But I am appalled at what I see right here tonight. I appreciate this good preacher and his prayer but, I, I [hesitation] in all honesty, I wonder about the facetious concepts that sometimes we, we, we go with. . . . I want to say as a pastor in this town that I think the time has come for sheer, clean, honesty. [applause] . . . All I ask, and I ask it as a Christian and I ask it as a citizen of this town, that this council quit playing [hesitation] patsy with some of the most important issues [hesitation] that could be. . . . If you're gonna pray [hesitation] then let's do it. . . . If you're sincere and honest about this thing about praying, okay, let's do it. But I do not like to see . . . I disagree wholeheartedly with this thing of bringing a prayer at a time like this, when I don't think this council has come to this session tonight [hesitation] in the attitude of prayer."

Milam's plea was in vain. The political leader had carried the day. The religious leader had ratified the decision--not just with an "Amen," but with an "Amen and Amen."

The promoters were up. So was cynicism.

I Favor a Vote, If . . .

Among those who favored a referendum, many thought that no vote would ever occur. Others assumed that even if a referendum occurred and Expo was defeated, "they" would go ahead anyway. Indeed, a *News-Sentinel* editorial in mid-May catered to and no doubt was purposely designed to stimulate and reinforce such sentiments. Even the UT student newspaper, the *Daily Beacon,* which had been most supportive of a referendum, was to spread the gloom. After the May 31 Council meeting, editor Barbara Ward wrote: "There's no reason to give up hope entirely."

With the proposed change in the finance plan, things were made even more difficult for the opposition. Their analyses still revealed city losses, although obviously not as dramatic as when the city was putting $11.66 million additional dollars into the project. But far more important were suspicions as to whether the new finance plan was a viable one. Was the new plan simply a smoke screen designed to get around the voters and the referendum petition?

Technically, in fact, the petition language was aimed at city money; and a ducking of city money hit the petition hard. Moreover, CBK leaders by now were aware that as a legal document the petition had serious problems even if city money were involved.

When CBK came into existence, it inherited the petition. In fact, as individuals, some of its members had raised the issue of the adequacy of the wording of the petition even before CBK was formed. No problem, we were told by Mrs. Hembree, by Urban League officials. The Urban League lawyers had looked at it. Even prominent Knoxville lawyer Boone Daugherty had looked at it, we were told. The issue was not pursued, which was CBK's biggest mistake in its five years of political activity.

Whatever might have been its legal deficiencies, however, a petition existed, ultimately with over 14,000 signatures. When combined with opinion poll data, the petition potentially was a potent political weapon. But to be a political weapon, mass opinion needs both quantity and intensity. The opposition had the quantity, but it was unable to maintain the intense and vocal support that was needed to overcome City Hall and the powers that be, the moneyed establishment of Knoxville.

The reduced intensity was demonstrated at the city council meeting of July 12. The Expo redevelopment plan was approved. With "assurances" of no city financial responsibility filling the air, the anti-referendum majority on council finally found themselves voting in a straightforward and direct manner against a referendum. The line was simple. Why yes, I was for a referendum. But now that the city is not risking any money, why should we have a vote?

Everything looked settled. Expo would occur at no cost and no risk to the city. It was in this atmosphere that elections for several city council seats were held in the fall.

Jean Teague's opponent was an ineligible candidate who lived outside the district. To the extent that Expo came up in her campaign, Jean hid in front of her record. There is no city money involved, and. . . .

Theotis Robinson was in trouble in his black district. He did what a smart politician does. He ducked the race. Shortly thereafter he became a vice president in the Expo Corporation. The evidence suggests that he did a better job for the promoters on council than as a vice president charged, among other things, with getting Black African countries to participate in Expo. Casey Jones, the ultimate winner in Robinson's district, was later to be another of those in favor of a referendum, if the city's financial support were involved.

Mrs. Willie Hembree, who had worked straightforwardly for a referendum, was defeated. She was getting old, and looked and acted it. She should have retired. Instead, she came up with a minimal campaign effort and was defeated--by Howard Temple, who was supportive of a referendum, if any city money were involved.

Rex Davis was another case with a straightforward record. Davis was the only straight shooter on the anti-referendum side. He was opposed to a referendum for a simple reason: he supported Expo. If a referendum occurred, he thought, Expo would be defeated. The Davis case belongs in every American government textbook. It perfectly fits the theoretical picture of how a system of representative government works. The representative gets his job, goes off to do his representing, and does a good job or a bad job. The folks back home know whether he did a good or a bad job, and vote accordingly in the next election.

Unfortunately for the theorists, the textbooks, and the American people, the representative usually doesn't want the folks back home to know what he does unless he thinks they will approve; and the folks back home aid the representative in his task by not looking too closely.

In the context of American politics, Davis may have acted too much like we think a representative should act and too little like the bulk of them do act. Davis was rewarded for his honesty. He was defeated in the primary.

The general election in Davis' district was won by Joe Mitchell. Mitchell would support Expo, but the number one plank in his platform said he would vote for a referendum, if the opportunity arose. Joe had his opportunity to so vote. He flunked the platform test, but he passed the establishment test. CBK just flunked. Its members had supported Mitchell in both the primary and the general election.

A Few Lies and a Fig Leaf

It was well over a year after the new finance plan was adopted in July 1977 before the opposition discovered that the plan had disintegrated months earlier. Suspicions existed all along as to whether the plan was real, and, if it was, as to whether it would work. Our suspicions had been based on two fundamental assumptions, which we viewed not as assumptions but as facts. First, neither the exposition nor the redevelopment component was a viable economic activity without large quantities of public money. Second, promoters hold an international exhibition not to take risks, but to make money. The question was: Could the carnival barkers con someone else into buying the bonds and taking the risk or would they themselves have to buy the bonds and take the risk?

Despite profuse assurances to the contrary from the promoters, the bonds could not be rated and could not be sold. To cover themselves, the promoters, in conjunction with the U.S. Department of Commerce produced still another finance plan. They turned to federal grants. And they turned back to the city. In other words, they put the risk back where it belongs for modern day "investors"--on the public.

Evidence indicates that this new financial direction had been secretly established at the latest by April or May 1978. The first inkling of a return to the city coffers, however, occurred in mid-August 1978 when David Massey, writing in an irregularly published neighborhood tabloid called *The Gazette,* reported that the Expo promoters had a plan to return to city council for an expected $8,950,000 in bonds.

When confronted with this information, which was based on an interview with a "source" in the U.S. Department of Commerce, the Expo Corporation wrote to city council: "You can be assured that in all discussions, negotiations and preliminary planning there have been no commitments on behalf of the Mayor and City Council." Tyree also pooh-poohed the report at the August 22 city council meeting: "It would be unfortunate if any organization is depending on the city for $8 to $9 million in bonds." Two weeks later at the city council meeting on September 5, he again denied the report in the course of providing council with what was billed as an interim financial report on Expo.

We subsequently discovered in U.S. government documents that four months earlier Tyree, in a May 4, 1978, letter to the Department of Commerce, had endorsed an Expo Corporation finance plan calling for at least an $8.95 million city commitment. Indeed, the endorsed plan provided for a city commitment of $21,235,000 plus interest of $26,318,000 over a 28 year period, if the federal grants did not come through.

The September 5 meeting had also involved another Tyree maneuver. Under questioning from Mrs. O'Connor regarding potential city commitments in federal grant applications, Tyree had promised that he would bring any applications for grants regarding Expo to council before their submission.

A month later, on October 3, we were back before city council with copies of a secret grant application to the U.S. Economic Development Administration (EDA). Tyree had signed the application on August 25, eleven days before his September 5th promise that such applications would be submitted first to council. On that occasion he had made no reference to the EDA grant. But there was more.

We now had before our eyes and before the eyes of city council a preliminary finance plan that was included in the EDA grant application. No longer was there only a telephone call, or the word of a Commerce official, or a report in a neighborhood tabloid. Instead, here on paper, in a document submitted by the city administration, was a finance plan that called for a city contribution of $10 million.

Moreover, the grant application, duly signed by the mayor, contained an explicit assurance from the city administration that city council had taken action "authorizing the filing of the application." In fact, however, neither city council nor the general public knew anything about the application.

Mark Thompson, a member of the Fourth and Gill Neighborhood Committee, as well as a member of CBK, had the audacity to observe at the October 3rd council meeting that "Mayor Tyree had been lying to us."

Tyree was furious: "You respect this office," he shouted, "do you understand? Don't call me a liar again." Mark was calm and collected, taking the flak from Tyree and from Councilman Bellah, who was also indignant over this display of disrespect for His Honor. "I'm trying to break the aura of secrecy that surrounds Expo," Mark said.

After the meeting Tyree apparently conceded to Larry Aldridge of the *Knoxville Journal* that a grant application existed. (Aldridge had a copy in his hand at the time.) But he went on to say that the city's contribution would be in the form of "in-kind" services, not a "cash outlay per se." The "cash outlay per se" came two weeks later.

In the meantime, President Carter had announced the awarding of a four-agency, $12.45 million federal grant package, a topic which receives more attention in chapter 4. When the promoters came to city council on October 17, 1978, with the finance package, the city was back in with its original $11.66 million contribution, initially passed in January 1977.

Surely we now had an interesting situation. First, it was clear that public opinion in the city had not changed. A UT College of Communications opinion poll in the spring of 1978, when in theory the city was not going to be risking taxpayers' money, had again revealed that an absolute majority of Knoxvillians opposed the exposition. Moreover, even with city money removed, 75 percent thought that a referendum should be held on the issue. A second interesting factor was that every sitting member of city council was on record as favoring a referendum if a city commitment was involved. Their past statements were a part of the record. Massey of *The Gazette* had documented it again. For the mayor, for council, it was time for a little mental gymnastics.

The city administration played it well. Think of all that federal money. True, it was said, we are going to borrow $11.66 million, but not by selling general obligation bonds. Instead, we will just be selling bond-anticipation notes. Aside from Bernice, the lines from council members were similar: I have said all along that if general obligation bonds are to be sold, I would vote for a referendum, but . . . . And not only that. Bonds will never have to be sold because the income from the sale of the land after Expo with other revenues will cover the $11.66 million.

"No risk" came on like a broken record--from the mayor, members of council, Expo's financial consultant, the city's bond consultant, and promoters. The city's bond consultant was bullish on the loan: the land will be "worth far in excess of the principal and interest paid to acquire the land." Six months earlier he had warned council about the dangers of additional bond sales. George Siler, the executive director of the Metropolitan Planning Commission (MPC), had no doubt that Expo "could put this city in strong financial shape in five years." (On October 16, 1978, the night before council's action, Siler, in presiding over a public hearing on the finance plan, ruled that the public could not ask questions. Only comments were in order. Back in March, as noted in chapter 1, he had been instrumental in postponing the RUDAT study of Expo. On October 27, he announced his resignation from MPC to become executive vice president of the Expo Corporation.)

The financial reality of the situation in October 1978 was simple. The city was back to square one, its original commitment. The amount of money was the same. The risk and obligation of the city were the same. The only difference: the money was being borrowed in the form of short-term bond-anticipation notes (that is, short-term notes sold in anticipation of a long-term bond sale) rather than long-term general obligation bonds.

Such facts were pointed out by the opposition. We had done our homework. We observed that the projected revenues of the promoters were inflated, that the projected expenses were deflated. We also said that the promoters would be back for still more money. We were later proven right on all accounts.

But right was not might. The opposition had opinion on its side, but it was a flimsy force. Cynicism. Defeatism. Lack of intensity. We were left with 14,000 signatures on a document that was legally defective. We had been overrun by hypocrisy and raw political power at home and in Washington.

The only man in the crowd was a woman. Mrs. O'Connor was the sole member of city council who raised any issues of significance at either the public hearing or the council meeting. Her motion for a referendum was hesitantly seconded by Milton Roberts, presumably to keep Bernice from being embarrassed. He should have joined the hypocrisy. The motion was defeated, 7-2.

For the public, council's consideration and justifications were a hoax. For the council, it was another fig leaf. For the mayor, it was a capital fig leaf. No payment of interest or of principal would be due until after the mayoral election, which was a year off. Indeed, almost all of the repayment process would begin in 1984, two years after Expo was over and, as it turned out, two years after Tyree's campaign for governor. The bulk of additional city commitments that were made in 1980 and 1981 followed the same pattern. Buy now; pay later--much later.

We Didn't Get Anything

There were three more events that occurred relative to the general issue of a referendum. One occurred during the gubernatorial election of 1978. The Democratic candidate was Knoxville Banker Jake Butcher. Butcher had taken leave from his position as Expo board chairman in order to campaign; but no one doubted that if he were elected, the full force of state support would be thrown behind Expo.

On the Republican side was Lamar Alexander, whose position on Expo fits the general nature of election campaign practices in the United States: if the issue is controversial, stay as far away as possible. On one occasion during the campaign, however, Alexander put out a feeler for the anti-Expo vote. In a Knoxville appearance toward the end of the campaign, he observed that he would support Expo, "if the people want it."

Already on the Alexander side because it didn't want Tennessee "butchered," the Expo opposition leaped at the feeler. In a letter to Alexander after his election success, CBK called attention to the 14,000 signatures on its petition and to the UT opinion polls. CBK also noted that in Knox County Butcher had been "soundly repudiated" in the election. The state should withhold its support of Expo until the city government could "demonstrate that the people of this city want this event to happen."

CBK did manage to obtain a session with Alexander to present its point of view; and the Alexander administration was distinctly cool toward Expo during 1979 and 1980. Even so, Alexander did offer some financial support to the exposition in 1979, although at a substantially lower level than the promoters' desired $20 million. No administrative official raised the possibility of conditioning that support on "if the people want it." (In 1981, the state became a major booster of Expo under the leadership of Commissioner of Tourism Etherage Parker and Governor Alexander himself.)

When the Alexander administration went before the state legislature in February 1979 seeking funds for what ultimately became the Tennessee Amphitheater, however, another potential for a referendum presented itself. CBK had been attempting to stimulate state legislators for some time. Finally a response occurred. It looked like a big one.

Middle Tennessee Democrat Tommy Burnett, majority leader in the House of Representatives, ripped into the proposed Expo support: "I could be a lot warmer toward Expo and the state pavilion if I knew . . . that it was not being crammed down their throats [in Knoxville]. If it takes the state legislature to force a referendum for Expo, so be it," he told a *Knoxville News-Sentinel* reporter in February. On March 23, he reportedly said that the promoters "don't want a referendum because they know it wouldn't pass," and on March 30 he stated that he would "probably try to require a referendum before the Assembly votes."

Then the "big" response faded with no explanation. The only known clues: Burnett talked on the phone with Jake Butcher on March 30, and he and House Speaker Ned McWherter had dinner with Butcher on April 17.

Burnett's about-face notwithstanding, his observations relative to Expo's lack of popular support in Knoxville were correct. A new College of Communications opinion poll was released on June 1. This 1979 poll revealed that opposition to Expo was essentially the same as it had been in 1977 and 1978. An absolute majority of 52 percent opposed the exposition. In fact, support for Expo showed a decline from 34 percent in 1978 to 27 percent in 1979. Even with over two years of Expo promotional efforts, expressed sentiment showed almost a 2-1 anti-Expo stance.

Such sentiment along with the upcoming election in October no doubt was part of the stimulus for another referendum call on Expo in September 1979. As formulated, however, the attempt for a referendum at this late date was not to be a vote on the existence or nonexistence of Expo per se, but rather on whether or not any additional bond money over and above the already authorized $11.66 million would be allocated for Expo.

The Expo people reassured the public and council: we are not going to ask for more money. But if you want to have a referendum, we won't oppose it. Indeed, the Expo board passed a resolution supporting "conscientious efforts for citizens to express themselves on this issue."

CBK members had thought all along that they were acting with the highest regard for conscience, even while they were experiencing wholesale secrecy and deception on the part of the promoters. In fact, on numerous occasions we had concluded that various members of the Expo crowd had no consciences to which an appeal might be made. The hypocrisy surrounding the board's "conscientious-efforts" resolution might be a case in point.

This conclusion was even more appropriate when we later discovered that only a few hours after the board's resolution was passed, another collectivity assembled behind closed doors at Jake Butcher's United American Bank Plaza. Reportedly, the group included Councilwoman Jean Teague, Expo executive vice president George Siler, and city law director John Roach. I suspect that other legal minds were there as well. The purpose of the meeting, whoever might have been in attendance, was reasonably clear: scuttle the referendum. If this is not possible, produce a referendum resolution that would so confuse the Knoxville voters that the bulk of them would vote contrary to what they intended, thereby allowing the Expo minority to emerge victorious in an election.

When Mrs. O'Connor appeared at the specially called council meeting on September 28, 1979, she was confident that she had the required votes needed to pass her resolution for a referendum on an emergency basis, thereby allowing the referendum to be placed on the November 15 general election ballot. The resolution was introduced. It seemed clear. Vote for additional support for Expo by voting "Yes"; vote against additional support for Expo by voting "No."

Almost before the echo of the "second" died out, a substitute resolution was introduced by Councilwoman Teague. The essence of the resolution was a reversal of the meaning of a vote. To vote against additional Expo support would require a "Yes," to vote for additional Expo support, a "No."

It was a slick maneuver. Bernice was able to smell a rat even before the mayor and other Expo promoters supported the Teague resolution. You're trying to confuse the voters, she argued. Nay, nay, responded Teague and the mayor. A barrage of words with no content followed.

Expo opposition forces desperately wanted to have even a limiting vote on Expo. But Bernice was right. Only a sophisticated, expensive campaign would make the issue clear to the voters. "Vote No On Expo" would be relatively easy. I responded to Teague and the mayor: "You don't think it would be confusing for Joe Dodd to go to the public and say, 'vote yes on Expo'? If the best you can do is Teague's motion, we don't want anything."

We won. We didn't get anything. Each resolution received a 5-4 vote, not enough for emergency passage.

The mayor was up for re-election. He was holy. Reconsider, he urged: "If somebody doesn't switch, then we don't have a referendum." Councilman Bellah was up for re-election. He too was holy: "I don't want to read in the paper that council voted down a referendum. They did not."

Bernice blasted back: "Council voted down a KIEE referendum. They must have stayed up all night working it up." She moved for adjournment. She too won.

The supreme irony had occurred. Every member of Council had voted for a referendum. (Don't say we don't keep our promises.) Yet no referendum occurred. "Smiley" Blanchard could really hold his head up high. He voted for "the people" twice.

After the meeting, Expo president S. H. Roberts, Jr., was asked for his response by the *Journal's* Larry Aldridge. "We would've favored Teague's resolution," he said. But a limitation on additional spending is really not necessary. "No one has requested additional funds and we have no intention of it," Roberts said.

The city later made additional direct, on-site commitments and expenditures of more than $22 million plus interest, plus whatever might be the cost of a promised city pavilion.

"If It's Going To Change the Town . . ."

Expectations of costs for the city were, of course, one of the reasons for opposing the exposition and seeking a decision by referendum. Knoxville had a strong, rapidly growing economy. No case could be made for a massive dose of public funds (so called pump priming) to stimulate economic development. Surely the public money required for Expo was more needed elsewhere. But other reasons for opposing the exposition existed.

The blockbuster urban renewal rationalization put forth by the promoters had long since been repudiated nationwide, precisely because tearing down everything in a 20- or 30- or 40-square block area in almost all instances meant a squandering of public resources. Tear down what needs to be torn down, leave up the healthy, and build around it. "Selective" redevelopment, CBK argued, is vastly superior to the total destruction approach, both economically and socially.

In Knoxville's case, we argued that it made no economic sense to tear down two modern medical clinics and drive 14 medical doctors out of the inner-city, or to drive two viable tire retailers out of the downtown area, or to destroy a new veterinary hospital. Admittedly a good portion of the Lower Second Creek valley was ragged and rundown, especially the railroad yard and the city's Clinch Avenue viaduct, but did that mean flatten everything and disrupt the operations of 62 businesses with 1,300 employees?

To the extent that Knoxville had economic problems, they were specific, not general. The needy were not wealthy businessmen and bankers. Rather they were people who in fact lived in the inner core of the city. The inner-city neighborhoods needed housing rehabilitation and far more attention devoted to their schools and recreational needs. Above all, they needed jobs. Would these needs be met by the exposition?

To the contrary. The city's concentration of resources on the exposition would take from the limited resources currently devoted to the neighborhoods. Expo created jobs would be largely of a temporary, moonlighting variety that would do little for the unemployment of the poor, the struggling, of the inner-city.

Such economic considerations, however, were not the only concerns of the opposition. What would be the social impact of introducing large quantities of people--better than 100,000 a day in July and August, the promoters estimated--into a city with a total population of 180,000 people? We saw increased crime and accident rates, increased air pollution, accelerated inflation, increased pressure on all city services.

We also saw disruption and congestion as a price that would be paid by the general population, especially in view of the inadequate plans of the promoters regarding parking. Significantly, the most direct impact of these items would be on the inner-city residents.

As this manuscript was moving to the printer in early 1982 the social-impact negatives left the abstract realm and hit concrete reality. "The enormous revenue available from overnight rentals," the *Knoxville Journal's* Ernie Beazley wrote in mid-February 1982, "has prompted the evictions of hundreds of Knoxvillians from their homes by landlords who want to clear their property for more lucrative Fair-time premiums." Greed fever was spreading like the plague more than two months before the exposition was to open. In the fact of what was a major calamity for many, city law director Jon Roach observed: "Most people realize there's a problem but the solution is somewhat elusive."

Were these kinds of negatives worth tolerating for the benefits that would follow Expo? Our answer was "no." Indeed, the so-called benefits burst from the mouths of the promoters so fast and furiously that a reasonable person had to question the entirety of the Expo package. And to the extent that there were benefits, they would flow into the hands of the few, the few who in reality needed so little, but had so much political power.

CBK chairman Leon Ridenour expressed our concerns well in an interview with freelance writer Russ Manning: We are talking about "a total change in our environment, the nature of this town afterwards. If it's going to change the town for everybody, I'd like to have a voice in the decision. Let us see what the total plan is . . . and then let us say whether we want to pay for it, suffer through it, and live with it afterwards."

Who? Me? Afraid?

The promoters' tendency to cover up, to duck questions about the total plan assisted in leading us to our conclusions. Indeed, the arrogance of the promoters regarding the question of free and open debate was perhaps as responsible as anything else for strengthening the resolve of the CBK hard core.

Although surely not always successful, the Expo promoters tried to control, to stage, their so-called public hearings in an attempt to sell the project to Knoxvillians in the winter and spring of 1977, after having already run it by "our" elected representatives. The promoters refused to engage in debate in a neutral forum. Regarding public debate with CBK, Expo president S. H. Roberts, Jr., said to Russ Manning: "I've got better use of my time than to spend time talking in front of groups with them." They were also inclined to duck other public sessions that might be uncontrolled. At the key city council vote on a referendum on April 5, 1977, for example, Councilman Milton Roberts wanted to know where the Expo people were. Mayor Tyree, who had led the charge against a referendum, stated: "They said they didn't want to turn the council meeting into an Expo debate."

The Expo leaders had a relatively simple perception of how to deal with political issues. You go to the people in power who can do things for you, and you convince them. And you do it under cover. You don't get city council members out in a public debate. You corner them.

The main promoters were major moneyed interests in the city. They had control over most of the formal political authorities and the bulk of the media. At the same time, the promoters knew that a majority of the people was opposed to their project. Should they give it all up because of a principle--even one called democracy?

The promoters, of course, were always quick to deny that they were afraid of a referendum. Indeed, during the course of almost three years of opposing a referendum, they always put forth other reasons why the people should not have an opportunity to make the decision on Expo. Not surprisingly, their reasons varied depending upon the situation at a particular time.

Mayor Randy Tyree, having a feel for the useful, had been in favor of a referendum during his campaign for mayor in 1975. Indeed, partly because of that promise I had accepted a magnificent four-by-eight-foot, double-sided plywood campaign sign with a portrait of Tyree on each side for my yard. Unfortunately, the sign was knocked over by a vandal or perhaps an intense partisan, thereby destroying a white pine that I had planted the previous Christmas.

A distinct possibility exists that I was responsible for a sufficient number of votes to cover Tyree's 396 vote margin of victory over incumbent Mayor Kyle Testerman. If so, I would be eligible for the *Guinness Book of World Records* as the owner of the most expensive $7 white pine that ever existed.

But I digress. The point, I believe, was that Tyree was not a rigid person regarding this campaign promise. As mayor he stepped in to lead the fight against a referendum. Others were capable of adaptation as well, although perhaps not as innovative as the mayor. (But, of course, we should expect more from a leader.) In any case, a number of reasons were cited for denying a vote by the people on Expo.

Perhaps the most frequently mentioned factor was money. If a referendum were held, the cost to the taxpayers would be $50,000. It was good to see that the promoters were interested in saving the public's money. It should be pointed out, however, that most of the moves for a referendum looked toward a vote at the same time as other elections, in which case no additional cost would have been involved. But even so, CBK chairman Leon Ridenour frequently was to observe that even a special election that cost $50,000 for an opportunity to stop a multi-million-dollar ripoff would be a bargain indeed.

A close second to money was time, a precious commodity that the promoters raised on their first appearance before city council when they beat back that request for a two-week delay in January 1977. If we wait for an election, the promoters argued, insufficient time will be available to acquire the property and sign up the corporate and foreign exhibitors. Regarding foreign exhibitors, Mayor Tyree was most explicit. On May 20, 1977, in arguing against a public referendum, he stated that commitments from foreign countries were needed within the next 60 days.

Significantly, the first offer for the purchase of property on the Expo site was not made until February 1979, more than two years after the Expo Corporation initially appeared before city council. The first commitment for a foreign exhibit was made by Italy on December 29, 1979, well over two years beyond Tyree's deadline, while the first domestic exhibitor, Baptist Ministries for Expo

'82 (with Mrs. S. H. Roberts, Jr., as secretary-treasurer of the group), was not secured until September 1980, an additional nine months down the pike.

Time indeed! It was a bad time for democracy.

"The Average Beer-Swizzlin' Citizen"

In weaker and less visible moments the promoters also relied upon the standard elitist arguments. Nancy Sharp quotes KCDC executive director John Ulmer: "You've got to look at who you're dealing with." City council, he observed, would explore both sides before acting, "but I'm not going to get that kind of time and concern out of the average beer-swizzlin' Knoxville citizen because he's going to go to the poll and vote mainly on hearsay and pull the trigger." Russ Manning quotes Ulmer as presenting a somewhat different angle. The average citizen would not only pay more attention to his beer than to the issue, but he would be "emotional" about it.

Ulmer no doubt was not alone with such thoughts. Nevertheless, others were a bit more discreet in making similar points. Mayor Tyree, Sharp notes, viewed Knoxville as a city with a negative bent, "voting against things rather than for them."

Tyree's observation falls flat on its face when compared with the results of a non-random opinion poll conducted by state Senator Victor Ashe in the spring of 1977. Of some 1,400 members of his constituency who responded to his request for information, 55 percent were against Expo. On the other hand, 67 percent favored establishing a unified city-county government, while an absolute majority also favored legalized gambling, neither of which indicates people who are unalterably opposed to change, or afraid of change, as was frequently alluded to by the promoters. The city is not automatically a "No" city, although we might want to acknowledge that under certain circumstances a negative vote might be a very positive thing.

The change in the finance plan in May-July 1977, which theoretically took the taxpayer off the hook, opened up another ideal reason for opposing a referendum. Tyree was reported to have observed: "I don't think that a referendum should be held because there is no front-end money from the taxpayer involved." In one form or another, the council members, aside from Mrs. O'Connor and Mrs. Hembree (who favored a referendum) and Rex Davis (who was opposed under any circumstances), fit into this category. It seemed like a safe position from May 1977 to May 1978.

But sometimes even safe ships aren't safe. Several months after this one had sunk, and two days before the promoters announced that, yes, they would come back to the city for money, Tyree started preparing the public. His argument was novel. In order to minimize its risk, he said, the city should own a portion of the site. He never explained how this could be the case. In any event, when no-city-money was lost, no-risk-to-the-city was found to replace it.

"It Would Have Been Voted Down"

My review of the events of 1977 indicates that of all the verbiage thrown out by the promoters there was only one meaningful reason expressed as to why they didn't want a referendum. It was put forth prior to the city council action deferring the referendum issue on April 5, 1977. The point was simple. The establishment of a referendum would jeopardize the April approval process by the Department of Commerce and the Bureau of International Expositions.

Indeed. That was the opposition's point--precisely. The approval process, we said, should begin with the people of Knoxville and then go to Washington and Paris. After all, bureaucrats in Washington and Paris were not the ones who would be paying the bills and suffering the consequences, whatever they might be.

Four years later in July 1981, one of the key promoters finally admitted precisely why no Expo referendum occurred. In an interview with the *Christian Science Monitor,* Mayor Tyree, the man who wanted "to have a little prayer about the kinds of decisions that we are going to make," stated that he had opposed a referendum because the exposition "would have been voted down." No promoter had ever before publicly made such a statement in Knoxville.

To the contrary, the promoters on several occasions claimed that they, in fact, were not opposed to a referendum. One of the most forceful of these statements was made in March 1977. As the *Knoxville Journal's* Ken Powers II reported it, a citizen at an Expo "information" session at Northwest Junior High "bluntly asked why Expo officials oppose a bid to let the voters decide the fate of the proposed exposition."

The response came from Rodney Lawler, a prominent Knoxville developer and chairman of Expo's Community Information and Involvement Committee. As Powers recorded it, Lawler emphatically stated that Expo officials did not oppose a referendum. "It would be un-American," Lawler said.

CHAPTER 3
"Give Light . . ."

"Bad for Business"

The place was Knoxville. The year was 1923. An enthusiastic municipal government reformer named Louis Brownlow had just arrived from Petersburg, Virginia, to become the head of Knoxville's new city manager form of government.

Brownlow observes in his autobiography *(A Passion for Anonymity)* that when he accepted the position he was "fully aware" that the government "had been corrupt, graft-ridden, dominated by political considerations--partisan, factional, and personal--and that the principal motivation for the conduct of the top ranks of the municipal machinery had been private gain for either the public officials or for their favorites in business, banking, and the professions."

When he arrived, the situation was even worse than he had imagined. He found not only graft and inefficiency but also smallpox. "I had thought that smallpox had been conquered," Brownlow recalled; but there it was in Knoxville, and plenty of it--"six or seven hundred cases in the pesthouse." He had kept up with the Knoxville news for some time before he arrived for his new job. But not one word about smallpox had appeared in any of the city's three newspapers. The reason for the void was simple.

"The newspapers and the business organizations," Brownlow states, had agreed many years before "that a smallpox scare would be bad for business."

"Bad-for-business" is a rather standard justification for censorship. Bad-for-politicians is another.

David Halberstam, in his *The Powers That Be,* offers the case of a young reporter with the *New York Times* named Turner Catledge, who had gone west in 1934 to cover Upton Sinclair's spirited campaign for governor against Republican Frank Merrian, the candidate of the owners of the *Los Angeles Times.* Catledge attempted to obtain some information about Sinclair's schedule from Kyle Palmer, the *Los Angeles Times'* chief political correspondent.

"Turner, forget it," Palmer responded. "We don't go in for that kind of crap . . . of being obliged to print both sides. We're going to beat this son of a bitch Sinclair any way we can. We're going to kill him." And, Halberstam observes, "they did."

Censorship, whether dictated by a government or otherwise imposed by the powers that be, runs directly counter to a core requirement and principle of a free society: the free and accurate flow of information. Principles of a free society aside, the evidence also indicates that manipulation of the flow of information is designed to serve the interests of the censors, frequently to the detriment of the interests of the larger society.

What Negatives?

The facts suggest that the flow of information in Knoxville during the Expo controversy suffered from a number of serious deficiencies. In part, we are simply back to promoters promoting by fabricating and distorting information, a process substantially aggravated in the Knoxville case by the existence of government officials as core components of the promotional effort. In addition, on far too many occasions the mass media, that institution the open society places so much faith in to counter such propaganda, simply failed to do its job. Indeed, to a substantial degree, the Knoxville media facilitated, even consciously served in some instances, the manipulation process. A case in point was the *Knoxville News-Sentinel,* by far the larger of Knoxville's two daily newspapers.

Many years of exposure to the local newspapers had left me with some general ideas about the basic orientation of each, but after having attended and participated in two of the Expo Corporation's "public hearings" in January and February of 1977, I became a bit more enlightened.

Although the *News-Sentinel's* coverage of both meetings had some resemblance to what actually took place, bias was obvious, with coverage of the second meeting being worse than the first. Many issues that seemed to be of core importance were either passed over entirely or barely mentioned. Puffy speeches from proponents were given extensive play. The situation became more objectionable during the first three weeks of March.

Ultimately I felt compelled to respond. I did so in a sharp letter to the editor on March 22. Other points were made, but foremost on my mind was the *News-Sentinel's* coverage of two recent meetings: one at Fulton High School on March 4 and the other at Austin-East High School on March 18.

In covering the March 4th meeting, the *Sentinel's* Bob Barrett wrote that members of the Fourth and Gill Neighborhood Committee "distributed question-begging sheets filled with statements of dubious authenticity designed to attack the project." I observed to editor Ralph Millett, Jr., that after such editorializing on the front page, his reporter had failed to mention in any way or manner the content of these statements of dubious authenticity. "Shouldn't the reader have an opportunity to judge Mr. Barrett's judgments?" I asked.

Contrast the *Sentinel's* coverage with that of the *Knoxville Journal*. The *Journal's* Ken Powers II had observed that Fourth and Gill "turned out with a printed list of questions criticizing the lack of a referendum, predicting further strains on city services and forecasting an unbearable increase in the costs of living." Powers continued by observing that the group "criticized the lack of guarantees on what will eventually be done with the Expo site and buildings and accused Expo officials of poor planning and making contradictory statements." The picture that emerged was substantially different from that of the *News-Sentinel*.

Two weeks after the Fulton session the Expo show had moved on to Austin-East High School and a predominantly black audience. Barrett was again on the scene and his story, sounding as if he were covering a harmonious dinner party, had as its title "Expo '82 Officials Enlist Blacks to Work on Plans." Although some suggestion of controversy was buried in Barrett's coverage, the *Journal's* Powers captured the real flavor of the meeting with a title of "Expo Officials Raked Over Coals." Powers indicated that aside from the usual questions about the lack of a referendum, the purpose of the community meeting, and who was behind the exposition, blacks ripped into Expo officials "for failing to involve the black community in the planning process and not insuring that the blacks will be able to take advantage of the economic opportunities."

Even before my letter to the editor concerning these meetings got in the mail, another Expo meeting had occurred. The coverage again fit the pattern.

That meeting at Northwest Junior High School involved controversy, even hostility. "Expo '82 Draws Mixed Reviews," the *Journal* headline read. Powers then went on to point out the issues, the controversies that arose before the crowd that "appeared to be evenly divided" between pro- and anti-Expo people.

The referendum issue was up again. At least two people questioned the adequacy of the $11.66 million city bond money for purchasing the 85 acre site. In regard to benefits, some asserted that "big business will take it all." Questions were raised about whether interstate improvements would be finished in time, about the adequacy of parking and transportation facilities.

The promoters, of course, had responses to these questions, and they appeared in the *Journal* story. And there were other presumed positives. The promoters' usual line was there: references were made to spinoffs like the state pavilion, the federal pavilion that will become "a self-supporting energy research center," and the public park that would be "maintained by a trust fund composed of the profits from Expo '82." The promoters also assured the crowd that "businesses will be encouraged to keep prices in line with pre-Expo levels through an organization such as the Better Business Bureau to control gouging and other predatory practices." In addition, the *Journal* carried a wide range of suggestions put forth by a member of the audience that covered the positive waterfront from labelling Knoxville "The Energy Hope of the Future," through the establishment of Amtrak service, to specific suggestions for energy research and tourist development.

The *News-Sentinel's* coverage of the Northwest meeting was a bit different. "Amtrak Line Among Suggestions for Expo '82," the headline announced. No indication of hostility appeared. The only suggestion of controversy was the line: "Questions continued about what would be in it for the little man." John Ulmer responded with the frequently told Spokane Cabbie Tale, the cab driver being quoted as saying: "It meant money in my pocket."

Otherwise, it was all glory. The remarks of that citizen speaker, identified as marketing director Jim Haggerty of a new advertising firm, were covered in detail. Comments from Expo team members John Ulmer, Charles Smith, and Rodney Lawler were covered. The story read like an Expo press release. Maybe it was; it had no byline.

Everything I had said in my letter to Millett was again confirmed. My question was now even more appropriate: "Has the *News-Sentinel* forfeited its right to be called a *news*paper?" I was not, however, to have the satisfaction of seeing my letter in print.

Nevertheless, the letter led to one of the strangest events of my five-year involvement in Expo. I received an apology from *News-Sentinel* reporter Bob Barrett, who had indeed seen my letter, even if it hadn't appeared in his newspaper's "Forum." The occasion was an April Fool's Day Expo "informational" meeting in the Fort Sanders community directly adjacent to the Expo site; but Barrett wasn't thinking "April fool." The lead paragraph of his story the following day referred to a meeting "filled with verbal fireworks." Indeed, on this particular occasion a balanced evaluation of Barrett's and Powers' coverage of the meeting would have to give the nod to Barrett. The problem had not been Barrett's ability, but rather the "line" of his management.

Perhaps my letter had struck a code-of-ethics nerve. (Whatever our editorial position, we need to be objective in our news coverage.) The preponderance of evidence suggests, however, that I more likely had touched a what-about-our-credibility nerve. (Damn, this is too obvious.) Whatever the case, the *Sentinel's* coverage of formal public meetings thereafter was far more competent. Indeed, the stories of writers such as Jan Maulden, John Moulton, Jan Maxwell Avent, and Bob Barrett himself were at least as balanced as those provided by the *Journal.*

Manage That "News"

Unfortunately for the people of Knoxville, the *News-Sentinel's* Expo role didn't stop with reporting what happened in public meetings. Numerous other ways existed for the *Sentinel* to boost the project, and its leadership exploited all of them, so much so that I ultimately began referring to the *Sentinel* as the "core propaganda instrument," the "mouthpiece" of the Expo Corporation.

My label wasn't designed to attack the *News-Sentinel's* use of editorial space. I surely would allow its editor substantial leeway with editorial opinions and still consider such action legitimate. *News-Sentinel* editorials took such leeway. Early in the game they attempted to put the stamp of progress and community good on the promoters and the stamp of narrow self-interest, negativism, and stand-patism on those who opposed the exposition. Editorials were used to defuse the opposition by suggesting that Expo would occur even if a referendum defeated the bond issue. Editorials were timed to pressure city council into rejecting a referendum, as well as to praise city council for being decisive, foresighted and brave in rejecting a referendum. Editorials were used to promote the appropriate candidates at the appropriate time. Indeed, on some occasions the *News-Sentinel's* editorials were quite creative, as illustrated by the one noted in the last chapter, in which the editor, with a few well chosen slaps at his typewriter, became the midwife of an Expo victory in a referendum.

The manner in which the *News-Sentinel* managed another part of the editorial page, however, was not to be labeled as legitimate. Letters to the editor are a crucial form of citizen participation in an open society. To some extent, the *Sentinel's* management must have agreed, because a substantial number of anti-Expo letters were run, including several of mine. (Indeed, an overwhelming majority of the Expo letters in both the *News-Sentinel* and the *Journal* were anti-Expo letters.)

Significantly, however, the sanctity of letters seemed to disappear at crucial junctures and for certain topics. Neither I nor CBK chairman Leon Ridenour, for example, could get a letter accepted before the gubernatorial election in November 1978. The same was true for the *Journal*, which, like the *Sentinel*, was supporting banker and Expo board chairman Jake Butcher in that election. At no time did the *News-Sentinel* accept letters that called into question its objectivity as a newspaper. And as time marched on and we arrived in 1981, the *Sentinel* management apparently placed a lockout on all my letters. Between March 23 and July 20, seven straight letters were rejected. Was it an accident, a series of split infinitives, or simply because they would be bad for Expo business? Were other citizens with serious comments about the exposition having the same experience? Here is the pitfall of letters to editors. Only the solitary writer and the newspaper management know what is rejected.

Even so, my own experiences along with those of others I personally know of are enough to enable a categorical statement: In its letters' policy the *Knoxville News-Sentinel's* management was solidly in the arena of controlled persuasion. Unfortunately, manipulation was not to stop with their letters policy.

Without doubt, the impact of a newspaper article is determined in part by where it appears in the paper. Placement bias seemed to be illustrated in a story of October 18, 1978, titled "Carter May Be Damaged by Aiding Butcher with Expo, ter Horst Says." This *News-Sentinel* story linked together the President of the United States, gubernatorial candidate Jake Butcher, Expo federal grant money, and syndicated columnist Gerald ter Horst. Ter Horst was President Ford's first press secretary and, quite notably, had resigned his post over a question of principle. One might have thought that the presence in a Tennessee city of a person who had committed such a rare act would be front page stuff in and of itself. The story appeared on page C-5.

Another case that illustrates the importance of placement bias occurred on June 22, 1981. After logging hundreds of lines over a period of more than two years concerning what appeared to be every possible potentially potential story about "the Russians are coming," the *Sentinel* almost forgot to tell its readers that the Russians had issued a conclusive "Nyet." The three-inch story appeared on page C-1.

Such a placement appeared to be a sign of the times, the times being those in which Expo was desperately trying to induce corporate exhibitors to climb on board. Negative news was not needed. Indeed, Terry McWilliams' *Journal* story about the Russians, although far larger in length and content, was relegated to page B-1. Nevertheless, it was prominently placed as the lead for the second section and could be seen without a magnifying glass. As the fellow used to say, "It's all relative."

Placement, of course, is not the only way a newspaper can cooperate in presenting the "proper" image. Sometimes masquerading as news was what I began calling "petite boosterism." It is boosterism because it is just that. It is labeled "petite" because it is characterized by so much enthusiasm, so much gushiness, that its ostentatious display of propaganda produces little positive effect for the propagandist (or at least I would like to think so).

Excellent examples of p.b. appeared in the *News-Sentinel* on April 29 and May 4, 1977, during the height of our campaign for a referendum. (Was the timing an accident?) The first was Barbara Aston-Wash's "Declaration of Expo '82," with a subtitle of "Energy--Of, By and For the People," while the second was Linda Felts Fields' "How Green Will Be The Expo Valley." For my purposes here, the gist of these articles should be clear enough from their titles, so I will obey my quivering stomach and refrain from offering summaries.

For those who think that truth-in-reporting is a value, a far more serious form of boosterism is "grande" boosterism. Unfortunately, it is much more subtle than the petite variety. It is more likely to have some news within it and appear in the "news" part (perhaps on the front page) of the newspaper. As a result, it is less easy to detect as boosterism.

Grand boosterism's key form is the press release of the interested party--in our case the Expo Corporation or some related agency such as the U.S. Department of Commerce. To be sure, press releases were not invented by Expo promoters. Indeed, the bulk of what we get out of Washington concerning the performance of our government is derived from a bureaucracy that is loaded with public relations personnel. In his excellent book on *How Washington Really Works*, Charles Peters cites a General Accounting Office (GAO) study as crediting the Department of Defense with having 1,486 such personnel. Members of the U.S. Congress get in on the act as well. "News" of their performances for the most part originates from within the offices of the congressmen themselves.

Whatever the agency or the individuals involved, whether administrative or elective, whether public or private, the issuance of a press release almost always has one fundamental purpose--to make something or someone look good. And to the extent that they can, those who release the press release like to have their press release treated as a "news" item rather than as a press release per se.

In this regard, the Expo promoters appear to have done quite well with the *News-Sentinel*. On the basis of content, numerous stories during the critical years of 1977, 1978, and 1979, suggest a press release tone. Only rarely was such an article identified as a press release. Most of them carried no byline. Occasionally, however, an authored story would display what seemed like the "proper" flavor. But the key question is not so much whether a story originated as a press release or was the "creative" work of a reporter. The issue is content. Does the story display the unquestioning, unwavering pro-Expo line? *News-Sentinel* business editor Laffitte Howard frequently provided this kind of "news."

A case in point was a story that appeared in the *News-Sentinel* on November 10, 1976. The title of "Energy Expo '82 Could Bring Better City Touring Leaders Told," was followed by the lead: "An exposition as exciting as all our tomorrows yet with the Old World gaiety of Tivoli and Ponte Vecchio and a flavor that will linger in better living for Knoxvillians.'' The incomplete sentence notwithstanding, the bulk of the article reads like a press release. It is written as a story covering a talk in Spokane and Seattle, Washington, with no dateline. The "proper" sprinkling of quotes from a talk by Expo executive architect Bruce McCarty appears in the story, which has no hint of a negative.

Other Laffitte Howard stories came forth in the following months, but one that seems particularly instructive appeared on May 29, 1977. The title was "Carnival or Catalyst: Words Express Hopes and Fears of Expo '82." The one sentence devoted to the "carnival" component is followed by the observation that "those who feel this way haven't seen the big picture. . . ." The remainder of the 14 column-inch story is devoted to the positive view of George Siler, executive director of the Metropolitan Planning Commission. Three months later Howard produced "Thoughts on Expo '82 Turning International," which turned to the views of Expo president S. H. Roberts, Jr.; but otherwise, it was more of the same.

Howard was consistent and persistent. On March 18, 1979, his "Expo Pledged $25 Million, Now Is Reality, Backers Say" appeared in banner headlines across the Sunday edition of the *News-Sentinel*. We acquired a copy of the press release that, according to David Massey of *The Gazette,* had been handed to Mr. Howard on the previous day. With the exception of minor adjustments here and there, plus a tacking on of several quotes at the end, Howard's story was essentially the same as the press release, except, of course, that it carried a by-line: "By Laffitte Howard, News-Sentinel Business Editor."

This story, like many others, was not generated by Expo for no reason. The promoters were in trouble and needed a public relations boost, especially at the local level. Although the story was written largely in the past tense, the promoters in reality did not yet have their money. Indeed, I was reminded of several so-called informational pieces that I had been exposed to when undertaking research during the Vietnam War. A number of official publications prepared by the United States Agency for International Development (USAID) were written in a manner designed to demonstrate past accomplishments when, in fact, a careful reading revealed that distinguishing between accomplishments of the past and hopes for the future was virtually impossible.

The Howard story must have been read closely and with a healthy degree of skepticism by *Knoxville Journal* reporter Ernie Beazley. Some two weeks earlier Beazley had reported "Expo '82 Financing Stymied." Then on March 17 he had written that the promoters were seeking pledges to back up an additional $2 million of up-front money from local banks before the national money-center banks would come into the picture. Indeed, when the glittering promotional aspects of Laffitte Howard's *News-*

Sentinel story are filtered through to expose the hard facts, it merely repeats the Beazley story.

It is doubtful, however, if more than a handful of readers penetrated the "positive" fog of Howard's story. And thus we see another way in which a captured press can be used. In this instance, an attempt was being made to cover up the earlier "bad" news. (Let's get a good face on it boys.) This was neither the first nor the last time the *News-Sentinel* would play such a role. In this case, however, the cover was not totally effective, at least for those who also read the *Journal*. Two days after Howard's story, Beazley again hit home with his "Banks: No Expo Commitments." The lead of his story, which was based on a new survey of bankers, went as follows: "Expo '82 promoters have not secured $25 million in credit needed to finance the energy fair nor have they extracted commitments for the financing, the *Knoxville Journal* learned Monday." Beazley had the audacity to call the bankers, and he came back with the quotes.

On the same day, the *News-Sentinel*, ignoring the Beazley story, came to the aid of its battered Expo friends by producing an editorial in which it praised the Expo Corporation "for being able to do its job." But, as David Massey of *The Gazette* was to note, the Expo Corporation, Laffitte Howard, and the *News-Sentinel* had been caught "with their pants down." *Journal* cartoonist Charlie Daniels was on target when he pictured, as Massey describes it, "a grinning Expo official exclaiming 'I've got the commitments in my hip pocket' but the official has no pants on! Lying nearby is the 'KIEE Press Release.'"

Thus, we find that once it went beyond the coverage of formal meetings, the *News-Sentinel* apparently saw its role as a promoting and supporting one. For its part, the *Knoxville Journal* also covered the formal meetings in a satisfactory manner, but its approach to Expo was substantially different from that of the *Sentinel*. To begin with, it was not as inclined to attribute as much importance to Expo's staged "public hearings" as the *News-Sentinel* did. And it was markedly less inclined to play the promotional, supportive role that so dramatically characterized the press-release philosophy of the *News-Sentinel*.

Simple Reporting Was Not Adequate

As for the television stations, we early had learned that the best that could be hoped for was a balanced treatment of "what we said" as compared with "what they said." And even that was not definitely to be expected from WATE (Channel 6), which was by far the most popular news station in the city. Indeed, our first outing into the world of press conferences told us something about WATE.

We were trying to attract a crowd to a city council meeting at which the referendum issue would be up. So we went before the media. We presented some of our substantive concerns about Expo economics. Primarily we wanted to get the word out about the council meeting. And we explicitly said so at the press conference. Well over a majority of city council was responding far more to the promoters than they were to popular opinion. Intense popular support for a referendum had to be demonstrated in order to obtain a popular vote on Expo '82.

On the evening news WATE gave us a bit of coverage, but then, whether knowingly or unknowingly is perhaps open to debate, reporter Jack Eisenhower demolished our efforts to encourage a public presence when he concluded by observing that this is a case of "too much, too late." City council, he noted, no doubt will vote for a referendum tomorrow night. City council, of course, did not vote for a referendum.

A few weeks later, Eisenhower was to demonstrate clearly his reluctance to step on the toes of the promoters. He passed on to me a vague threat from some obscure "they": "You'd better watch yourself."

Eventually Eisenhower was on his way to Nashville to another station, but insofar as stepping out on the Expo issue was concerned, no significant improvement occurred with his followers. We were to have some brief shots at the promoters on the early morning (6:00 a.m.-7:00 a.m.) "Today in Tennessee" talk show, but as for an aggressive news perspective, WATE's management had early set the pace for its staff through its open editorial line as an unabashed supporter of the exposition and a harsh critic of the referendum forces. Although the much-less-viewed Channel 10 and 26 news programs were more inclined toward balance, they were not motivated to go beyond the simple reporting that is generally characteristic of local TV news.

Where then was Knoxville to find a hustling, observing, questioning force to stem the tide of Expo propaganda? The *News-Sentinel* was out. Television news was out. Even more clearly, the city government was out.

Very early in the game the late professor Arnett Elliott, of the University of Tennessee's political science department, had tried to schedule a meeting with Mayor Tyree for a delegation from our group. When Elliott indicated that we wanted to talk to the mayor about *not* supporting the exposition, Tyree's office aide stated, as reported by Nancy Sharp, "Really, it's too late for that." The aide refused to arrange an appointment.

But such a denial was not necessary to demonstrate the mayor's position. As a regular feature of any Expo Corporation public-relations stunt, city administrators, including the mayor, were out in force, proclaiming the no-risk, all-glory line, even to the point of lying about the compatibility of Expo plans with the existing plans of the city, especially with regard to city street and highway improvements.

The gist of the matter boiled down to this: I had very early arrived at the conclusion that if aggressive investigative work was to occur regarding the potential negative impact of Expo, it could only come from two sources. One was Citizens for a Better Knoxville, the group of which I was a part. But clearly, we did not have the resources to handle the job. That then left the *Knoxville Journal.*

Hoping for the best, I wrote a letter to the *Journal* editor William Childress on March 25, 1977. After complimenting him on the *Journal's* prior coverage of open meetings, I noted that a proposal of the magnitude of Expo deserved considerable coverage, including objective critical evaluation. Simple, passive coverage of public events was not adequate. Instead, what the public interest required was independent, investigative reporting. Neither the mayor nor any other part of city government was going to do any investigating. And surely nothing could be expected from the *News-Sentinel.* "If the job is going to be done," I said, "more than likely it will have to be done by the *Journal.*"

A partial listing of deserving topics was provided. We needed, I suggested, the reality of: "The Spokane experience during and after their exposition; traffic flow and parking (or lack thereof), given the projected increase in cars; impact on city services; expectations concerning increased criminal activity; changes in air quality; and taxation increases during and after Expo as a result of Expo itself." Thus far, I indicated, our information on such items had been obtained from the promoters themselves. This, for obvious reasons, was not adequate.

The letter was so much paper. If read, it had no impact. A personal session with the editor was friendly but apparently of no more consequence. I argued that Expo was big, an important issue before the community, and deserving of detailed and continuing coverage by a reporter assigned exclusively to the topic.

The critical year of 1977 continued . . . and passed.

Early 1978 saw the appearance of a city grant application to the Department of Housing and Urban Development (HUD) for an Urban Development Action Grant (UDAG). The UDAG application contained a number of false claims. Supposedly, the city had conducted public hearings that had allowed the people a voice in putting the application together. Supposedly, city council had approved the submission of the application. Both actions were legal requirements. But the city had stepped out quickly trying to find money. No time was available to deal with such niceties. (The same UDAG application also made certain financial commitments for street improvements if the grant were approved. No public discussion of such commitments had occurred either.)

The city "lied," said a spokesman for the Inner-City Neighborhood Coalition (INC), a group of twelve inner-city neighborhood committees.

In a simple reporting sense, the media covered what we said, what the mayor said in response. But there were no investigative activities, no documents researched, and as a result no independent coverage of the controversy. We were on solid, unshakable ground, and the mayor was grasping at straws. But for all the public knew, the controversy was just another hot-air contest. If we won, it was merely an instinctive reaction: "Hell, he always lies."

Early 1978 also saw the emergence of another major document. Under contract with the city's redevelopment agency, Knoxville's Community Development Corporation (KCDC), and the Expo Corporation, Economic Research Associates (ERA) produced a two-volume study; one dealt with the "Economic Feasibility of Energy Expo '82," while the other dealt with the "Development Potential of Lower Second Creek." These two volumes were the economic justifications for Expo and its related post-Expo redevelopment plan. In theory, they were to provide the supporting base for a sale of $46 million in bonds. They looked like something for the media to chew on.

My spring break at the university was devoted to producing a thorough, critical analysis that roasted the ERA performance with respect to hopelessly inflated projections regarding particularly the post-Expo redevelopment that ERA said would occur on the site. For release with the ten legal-size pages of the critique I prepared a one-page summary. The summary was duly summarized by the press. The *Journal's* coverage appeared on page 20. To its credit, the *News-Sentinel* ran a story on page one. But I suspect that few, if any, reporters read either the ERA analyses or my full critique of them. Surely no evidence exists to suggest that any reporter tried to look at the documents for purposes of evaluation. Apparently, however, at least some members of the board of KCDC did read the critique, which may have had a substantial influence in steering the board away from approving the sale of the $46 million bond issue.

"It Was Embarrassing"

The only blight on the timid-press horizon came from *The Gazette*. In its August-September 1978 issue, *The Gazette* had a twelve-page insert on Expo. In part it was opinion, with articles by pro- and con-participants. But the core of the special supplement was first-class investigative reporting by David Massey. With partial support from the Fund for Investigative Journalism, Massey had been so bold as to contact not only those in favor and those against Expo but also Department of Commerce officials, HUD officials, railroad officials, and the professional real estate appraiser who supposedly had appraised the cost of acquiring the Expo site. The titles told the stories: "Expo Headed Back to Council: Secret Finance Plan Contains GO [general obligation] Bonds," "Property Appraisals: 'Just a Damn Guess,'" "Expo's Got Those Southern Railway Blues," "Carter Wanted to Know: Why HUD Said 'No' on UDAG."

In all essential respects Massey was correct: Expo did come back for city money; dramatic cost overruns occurred in property acquisitions, so much so that the city was able to acquire only some 30 acres of the 80 acres it had intended to buy; the Southern line continues to run through the middle of the valley; and Carter's pressure on HUD (and other administrative) officials ultimately was to tap the federal money tree, regardless of procedural requirements.

A reporter from the established press observed to me that "it was embarrassing" to have a neighborhood newspaper covering the news while the major dailies stood on the sidelines. But this observation aside, *The Gazette* had little impact.

Unlike Expo press releases, *The Gazette's* articles were not copied for redistribution by the "legitimate" press.

The year 1978 continued . . . and passed.

But the News Hurt Too Much

In appearance, the Expo project again was on solid ground in early 1979. Referendum moves had been defeated. Federal ($12.45 million) and city ($11.66 million) money had been approved for site acquisition, relocation of businesses and residents, and improvement of the site. Supposedly $25 million in private up-front money for the Expo Corporation was just around the corner. In December the U.S. Government had officially issued invitations to the foreign countries, urging their participation. Wasn't it all go?

At this point, over two years into the Expo controversy, we find several factors coming together to produce a spirit of investigative activity that was to continue for seven months. It poured forth from the *Knoxville Journal's* Ernie Beazley (now a reporter with the *Wall Street Journal*). The beginning came in February 1979 when I found myself in possession of new appraisals of the value of 17 (of a total of 151) parcels of property on the Expo site. Collectively, these appraisals, which were to be the basis for KCDC's initial offers to purchase the property, were two and a half times the earlier estimates.

This was cost overrun news of the first order. We had the facts. But what could we do with them in the context of Knoxville's media? After assessing the possible disclosure routes, Leon Ridenour and I settled in on Ernie Beazley, even though neither of us knew much about him. Indeed, essentially we knew only one thing.

During Jake Butcher's campaign the previous fall, Beazley on one occasion had covered a Butcher fund raiser at the Hyatt Regency Hotel. A short time before, President Carter, with Butcher and Senator James Sasser in attendance, had announced $12.45 million in grants for Knoxville's exposition. Because of some of our activities, however, the *Washington Star* was close to the story and printed two long stories concerning procedural irregularities regarding the grants.

Beazley asked Butcher if the stories would hurt his campaign. Butcher, Beazley reported, wasn't concerned that the Economic Development Agency hadn't yet approved the grant. He followed some cocky remarks with something that at least touched on arrogance: "I'm going to have this kind of influence over the President when I'm governor that I've got now."

Few reporters in Knoxville wrote about Butcher in any form. To my knowledge, none wrote in an unapproving fashion--except Beazley, one time, in one story. We got the information to him, and he was off and running on this and a multitude of other Expo issues. In addition to site acquisition cost overruns, there were problems with federal funding; state funding; private funding; relocation overruns; KCDC secrecy regarding property appraisal and acquisition information; acquisition of railroad property; internal financial revolt; and on one occasion, insufficient funds to cover Expo's payroll. Even as the *News-Sentinel* struggled to cover Expo's thrashing tracks, the word was spreading.

In perhaps his most important story, Beazley in August 1979 revealed the personnel composition of Hall-Sledge and Co., a firm that had been hired as a financial consultant by the Expo Corporation the previous February. U.S. Securities and Exchange records indicated, Beazley reported, that Hall-Sledge's stockholders included United American Bank chairman "Jake Butcher's brother-in-law, four UAB attorneys, two UAB directors, two former vice presidents of the bank and the wife of a current vice president." It was a 100 percent Butcher connection in ownership and operation.

Apparently Beazley's end runs through the months from February to September 1979 were not undertaken without encountering opposition from the *Journal's* management. But the stories kept coming. Toward the end of the period, however, the promoters were getting increasingly jumpy. It was getting late. Something had to happen. Finances had to be solidified. The bad news was hurting.

Beazley reported on August 24 that the Expo Corporation "had formed a panel to promote more 'positive' news about the exposition." The panel, which we dubbed the Positive News Committee, was headed by none other than Roger Daley, president and business manager of the *Knoxville News-Sentinel*.

Perhaps the promoters knew what was up. On the outside, at least, some evidence existed to suggest that for all its political potency at home and in Washington, the Expo project was being threatened by too many people knowing too much about the real Expo. Abruptly the Beazley stories stopped.

What had stopped Beazley?

The evidence was skimpy. Immediately prior to his silence, he was engaged in putting together a major conflict-of-interest article in which he was identifying the who-gets-what component of exposition gravy. The article never appeared. I had earlier talked to *Journal* editor Bill Childress. I didn't think he had spiked Beazley. Moreover, several sources suggested that the *Journal*, at the time a privately owned paper with a predominantly Republican-oriented editorial line, had endorsed Democrat Jake Butcher in the 1978 gubernatorial election over the objections of Childress. Presumably, that could only be done by *Journal* publisher and owner Charles H. Smith III. We had our suspicions, but. . . .

With Success Comes Failure

Beazley had been spiked for better than a month when the *Reader's Digest,* in its November 1979 issue, put forth a resounding critique of the Expo project. Upon his return from a foreign assignment in early 1979, senior editor Kenneth Y. Tomlinson of the *Digest's* Washington Bureau had run across two articles in Time Incorporated's *Washington Star* that had been stimulated by shenanigans associated with Carters' $12.45 million grant announcement.

Although finally prompted by Carter's indiscretions, the authors of the *Star's* initial article had been looking for some time for a national angle on which they could "peg" a major Expo story. The early interest of Rudolph Rauch III and Richard Woodbury had been produced by the dogged determination of CBK chairman Leon Ridenour to get something going with the national media. By the time Carter acted to boost Expo and the gubernatorial prospects of Jake Butcher in late 1978, Ridenour had been in contact with *Time* magazine's Atlanta bureau for over a year, feeding to Woodbury all information that might stimulate *Time* to step into the picture. Woodbury had become interested enough to come to Knoxville for a look and several interviews. But because of the tremendous competition which exists for space in the weekly magazine, Woodbury couldn't get a story past the New York editors.

The Carter connection produced the necessary national peg, but again it was not sufficient for *Time's* demands. As a result the cover-the-Expo-waterfront story ran on the front page of the October 11, 1978, *Washington Star*. Although reference was made to the Carter connection, the article fundamentally was a wide-ranging, 40-column-inch analysis of Expo itself.

By November 1, *Star* reporter Anthony Marro had pulled together the loose ends of the Carter connections with Butcher and with the federal agencies. The facts were presented in another front page story, this time of better than 60 column-inches. Marro had covered the ground thoroughly and effectively. In spite of his anti-pork-barrel rhetoric, Carter looked like a wardheeling politician helping out his buddies from Tennessee.

Leon had stimulated the national media. Indeed, the November 6th edition of *Time,* on the stands before the Tennessee gubernatorial election, drew on the earlier *Star* articles and some thoroughly documented investigative work on Butcher's banking practices by the *Commercial Appeal's* (Memphis) Lewis Nolan to produce a short but pointed article entitled "Jake Butcher: Another Lance?" with a subtitle of "A 'Treasure,' Says Carter."

It was information of this kind that prompted the *Digest's* Tomlinson to call me. After several trips to Knoxville, numerous interviews with pro- and anti-Expo elements, and a thorough grounding in the printed background, Tomlinson was in tune with the situation. But he was waiting for a decisive "it's go" or "it's no" on the fair itself. The wait was long. Apparently too long. Ultimately, Tomlinson decided to run his story without the decision. It was a blistering attack on the project and the Carter-Butcher connection.

"Expo '82 is apparently a boondoggle that will not die," said Tomlinson.

Even before the November *Digest* hit the stands in Knoxville, both newspapers were on the attack. Perhaps because Tomlinson had depended heavily on Ernie Beazley's articles, the *Journal* was even more defensive than was the *News-Sentinel.* Indeed, the *Sentinel* story at least carried the general substance of the *Digest* article. The *Journal's* critique was a no-content blast.

My worst fears about the *Journal's* future Expo coverage had been confirmed. I prefaced a letter to editor Bill Childress with "This letter gets a little rough."

And it did. I pointed to the fact that the *Journal's* October 18 story, titled "Reader's Digest Article Unfair to Expo '82," never got around to saying why the *Digest* was unfair. "Could it be that the Expo Corporation's Positive News Committee, headed by *News-Sentinel* Business Manager Roger Daley, now dominates the *Journal* as well as the *News-Sentinel?*"

The brief letter concluded with a very brief paragraph: "Over the past few weeks numerous people have asked me: 'What happened to the *Journal?*' Most questioners don't really need an answer." The letter didn't get to *Journal* readers.

The *Reader's Digest* article, my letter, or anything else notwithstanding, it was already too late to stop the exposition. We had needed investigative activity and public awareness in 1977 and 1978. CBK had kept plugging away, but the fall of 1979 was simply too late, especially with no Knoxville media source on the job. After Beazley, Expo was back in command of the Knoxville media, and, as time went on, of itself as well.

On October 12, 1979, the promoters signed a loan agreement that involved 43 banks, ranging from Knoxville to East Tennessee, to regional centers such as Nashville, Atlanta, and St. Louis, to the biggie, Chemical Bank in New York City. As we perceived it, the only major obstacle the promoters had to overcome besides a tendency to fall over their own feet was funding for the federal pavilion, which we assumed, rightly as it turned out, was a precondition for the actual flow of money from the national money center banks.

We had developed some contacts in 1979 among staff members of U.S. Senators Lowell Weicker of Connecticut and Ernest Hollings of South Carolina, both of whom were on the Senate appropriations subcommittee that was responsible for Department of Commerce funding, and as such a key link in the U.S. pavilion money chain. Nevertheless, we were fighting a losing battle. The promoters had their local power base; they had Tennessee representatives in the U.S. House of Representatives; they had Senators Howard Baker and James Sasser; they had President Carter; they had the back-slapping, pork-barrel system that is so well established in Washington.

The promoters fumbled a few times, but with much clenching of teeth and moaning about how difficult the task was, they finally stumbled backward over the goal line. The U.S. Senate ended the promoters' agony when it effectively concluded the U.S. pavilion funding process on June 29, 1980. World peace and energy solutions were finally on their way.

Meanwhile, all the local media had gone back to the simple reporting process. Life in Knoxville was again on an even keel. It was to remain so until mid-August 1980, when another burst of sunshine penetrated the Expo cloud of secrecy.

Try Again

The city had again gone the federal grant route, and an attempt to obtain a $15.75 million grant from the UDAG program was finding more receptive ears in Washington than had the earlier application. We had followed the grant process closely even before the application was filed on April 30, 1980, and were aware that the city's application again had a number of serious problems, including phony investor information. We had so advised the Department of Housing and Urban Development (HUD) and supplied them with facts and figures and a large quantity of supportive evidence.

Regarding President Carter's earlier $12.45 million, four-agency grant package, CBK and an assortment of other groups and individuals had filed a federal suit in February 1979 in which we charged, among other things, that violations of grant regulations had occurred. But a lack of funds to pursue the case had forced us to withdraw the complaint less than four months later. During that period the federal agencies had been concerned about dotting "i's" and crossing "t's." But once the threat of the suit was gone, they were much less vigilant and were anxious to get back to business. And business for the HUD UDAG administrators was giving away money. Otherwise there would be no UDAG program. The chain continued: no UDAG program; no UDAG administrators. As a result, we didn't expect much reaction even as we passed on our complaints to HUD during the Spring of 1980. (There was a reaction for the promoters, however, when a HUD grant of $9.9 million was approved on July 2, two months after the application had been filed.)

CBK, hoping to stimulate some investigative reporting, had also advised media sources that the grant application had muck in it that could use a raker. The *Knoxville Journal,* in spite of its faults, still had to be it, if anything was to go at a meaningful level in Knoxville. In addition, another source had developed that at least had a base within the state. This was the *Tennessee Journal,* an opinion weekly out of Nashville that was published by a former associate of Winfield Dunn, Tennessee's Republican governor from 1971 to 1974.

The *Tennessee Journal* had already shown its interest with two substantive, nonpuff articles in mid-1979. Now it came forth with another on August 11, 1980. On the 12th and 13th, the *Knoxville Journal* also poured it out, again from the typewriter of Ernie Beazley, after almost a year's absence from the Expo beat. Collectively, the three stories, through hard-hitting, investigative reporting, unraveled not only some of the shenanigans in the grant process but also substantial additional information about the directional flow of Expo "opportunities." All economic roads led not to Rome, but rather to Knoxville, Tennessee, at the corner of Main and Gay, the home of United American Bank and its board chairman, Jake Butcher, who was also the board chairman of the Expo Corporation.

As will be seen in chapter 4, these stories dramatically increased the information available regarding the real meaning and force behind the exposition. And we had something that could be passed on to an increasingly interested national media. Media-wise, this was the most encouraging thing that had happened to us in a long time.

On August 18 the *Tennessee Journal* observed that Beazley's *Knoxville Journal* stories had followed "the recent death of *Journal* publisher Charles Smith III, lending credence to the charge by some Knoxvillians that Smith had personally blocked the accounts [of questionable Expo-related matters] earlier." The *Tennessee Journal* also reported that *Journal* editor Bill Childress had said that "neither Smith nor he ever ordered the Expo stories stopped. . . ." Reality? Perhaps time would produce a partial answer.

Real Reporting by Real Reporters

Would the August exposé be but a passing breeze in Knoxville's polluted air? In the short run the answer was yes. For two months Expo puff stories were prominent in the *Journal's* Expo coverage. Then in November 1980 the *Journal* did what I had urged Childress to do almost four years before. A reporter was assigned exclusively to the Expo beat. He was Terry McWilliams, a new reporter in town who went at it--in his own quiet, easy-going style. He covered and covered thoroughly Expo accomplishments. But he was not simply a stenographer for rosy Expo press releases. All was not rosy.

Large numbers of visitors would have a dramatic impact on city and county public services. McWilliams dug into issues concerning increased demands for emergency ambulance and hospital services, fire protection, management of the flow of traffic, dealing with expected increases in criminal activity, etc. McWilliams, that is, provided in-depth information on a number of topics that the opposition needed the public to be aware of in 1977 and 1978.

But the information was also needed in 1980 and 1981--if the powers that be were going to feel sufficient pressure to provide for increased needs at a more or less decent level. Would they rise to the occasion or would they "wing it," leaving the members of the general public to handle it as best they could?

For the most part, McWilliams' stories revealed tentativeness--regarding not only the provision of services per se but also in the planning for providing services. Many references were made to costs--and to money, or rather lack thereof, and to possible federal grants. Tentativeness was still there, as this was written four months before the fair was to open.

McWilliams did not stop with services. He also dealt with complaints from the unemployed regarding a rather simple question: Where are all those jobs that were promised? He uncovered internal Expo management problems, hit at problems of redevelopment after the exposition, raised issues regarding the construction timetable of the federal pavilion, and pointed to the lack of a residual use for the pavilion, as UT was ultimately forced to announce publicly that the building was inappropriate for post-Expo usage as an energy research center.

Mcwilliams, however, did not have all the action. Quite by accident, an article in the *Atlanta Journal* by Evan Kossoff passed our way in mid-October 1980. Unknown to Knoxvillians, corporate exhibitors were being extremely slow in jumping on the Expo bandwagon. The Atlanta article was followed by a thorough, detailed study--with charts of who was, who wasn't, and who was undecided about coming--by Bob Jones and Cynthia Moxley of the *Knoxville Journal* on December 5. The fair's theme might be energy, but few of the major energy producers were going to provide exhibits. It was not a pretty picture of the promoters or their success. And it became even less pretty when lagging corporate participation joined nagging Butcher shenanigans in a *Wall Street Journal* front page story on December 29, 1980.

Cynthia Moxley asked Mayor Tyree if the *Wall Street Journal* article would have any negative impact on signing up corporations for exhibits. No, said Tyree. How so? said the reporter.

"Businesses," Tyree stated, "are not influenced by newspaper reports because they consider the source." Whereupon Moxley observed that the "source" was the *Wall Street Journal,* a well-respected business daily with a circulation of 1.8 million. The *Knoxville Journal* seemed to be back in tune. It was calling a spade a spade.

On March 21, 1981, the *Journal's* Bob Jones returned with superb coverage of the GAO's blistering "costly-mistake" report on the federal pavilion. Another *Journal* reporter, Susan Tremblay, did the first price-gouging story regarding hotels and motels on May 15.

By this time the *Journal* shakeup which had followed the death of its owner and publisher the previous summer had worked itself out. The paper was sold to Gannett, a national newspaper chain, in the spring of 1981. Coverage of Expo continued. It might not have been the best, but it was the best thing in town. Indeed, as 1981 continued to unfold, Ernie Beazley was back.

Beazley burst forth on October 9 with a burning roast of hotel-motel, price-gouging room rates in an article ("Fairtime Room Rates Shoot Through Sky") which also included coverage of an attempt to cover up and rationalize the real picture by Knoxvisit, the local tourism promotion agency. On November 2, Beazley hit again with a similar story on campground fees ("Campsites to Peg Doubled, Tripled Rates During Fair").

Beazley was also back looking at the Expo political process. In a long story on October 9 he reported the events surrounding Senator William Proxmire's charge that the National Aeronautics and Space Administration (NASA) had attempted to pressure firms that held contracts with NASA into sponsoring and paying for a $5 million space pavilion at the Knoxville World's Fair. Expo president S. H. Roberts, Jr., "under NASA tutelage," had met with aerospace contractors and not only passed the hat but also spelled out the dollar amounts, ranging for the various firms from $1 million down to $250,000. (No doubt, it was a "fair-share" plan.) Proxmire had written to NASA administrator James M. Beggs: "Your actions are a serious breach of the arms-length relationship that should exist between the federal government and the firms with which it does business." In responding to the charge, Beggs quite naturally justified his actions by citing the national interest.

Proxmire was successful. The space pavilion didn't lift off.

Less than a month after the Proxmire NASA story Beazley, in a copyrighted story on December 2, 1981, got inside Expo financial operations when he reported on the contents of the Expo Corporation's Internal Revenue Service (IRS) file.

Was there a reason for supporting Expo in the early days? Expo master architect Bruce McCarty had some reason. During a 12-month period in 1979-1980 McCarty's firm received $717,133 for professional services. KIEE's legal counsel, Robert F. Worthington, partner in a law firm that includes Senator Howard Baker, had received $153,342 for the same period. Executive consultant King Cole, the former president of Spokane Expo '74, was paid fairly well for his expertise, when he received $111,678. And Expo financial consultant Hall-Sledge, that firm made up entirely of members associated with United American Bank, received $258,848 for its assistance in arranging Expo's private loan.

Was there a reason for supporting Expo at the seat of the nation's government? While the Expo opposition was nickel and diming it, largely with letters and phone calls to HUD and Commerce officials and congressional committee staff members, the Expo promoters were approaching congressmen and bureaucrats somewhat differently. Public information already existed concerning a large number of the promoters' personal and written contacts with such officials, a substantial part of which was accomplished at public expense by Knoxville city officials and paid city consultants. Now Beazley added to the picture.

Expo's lobbying efforts "during a 24-month stretch in 1978-1980" had cost a cool $146,515, with almost all of the money going to "a prominent Washington-based lobbying firm" headed by Robert Keefe, a former Democratic National Committee official. In an interview with Beazley, Keefe stated that KIEE had averaged paying his firm about $60,000-$65,000 yearly. "We've been involved with the fair since May 1977 in Washington, whether it was lobbying Congress or helping government agencies package funds for the fair," he said.

Beazley's story even had some new information about the Knoxville media.

Early in the game, CBK had obtained a document in which Roger A. Daley, business manager and president of the *Knoxville News-Sentinel,* was listed as a member of the board of directors of the Expo Corporation. We also knew that during the time of financial troubles in late summer of 1979 the Expo Corporation had formed its "Positive News Committee" with Daley as its head. Now Beazley had more. Expo's IRS file revealed that among the contributions the Expo Corporation received during the 12-month period ending on March 31, 1980, were a $1,000 gift from the former *News-Sentinel* assistant business manager Gil Champagne and another $1,000 from Roger Daley.

It had been a nice day's work for Beazley.

In all fairness it must be acknowledged that occasionally *News-Sentinel* reporters also did "a nice day's work." Bob Hetherington's excellent coverage on February 8, 1981, of post-Expo redevelopment problems has been mentioned earlier. John Moulton, although over two months after Tremblay's *Journal* article on the same topic, hit hard on July 30, 1981, with detailed information regarding "Rates at Many Motels Expected to Soar for Fair," but his story was run on page 8, thereby leaving Beazley's stories three months later as the ones that drew a dramatic reaction.

(Actually Beazley's stories were to receive prominent attention for reasons aside from placement. One item was his charges against Knoxvisit. Another was Knoxvisit's reaction, which led to new coverage by Beazley as well as an editorial by the *Journal*. Several letters-to-the-editor were printed. Other media elements got into the act. As price gouging moved up on the public agenda, the Expo Corporation, the mayor, and even the University of Tennessee administration flailed away at the gougers, being careful, however, not to tarnish the city's image. Reference was made to "the few" who were giving "the many" a bad name. In fact, however, "the few" were quite "many." Moreover, as I was to note in a set of letters to the *Journal*, the Expo Corporation was surely the first gouger with its concessionaire lease prices, and perhaps the leading gouger otherwise with its general-admission ticket and funland-ride prices.)

Perhaps "Archie Campbell Sez" offered the last word on gouging. Archie's contribution to the December 12, 1981, *Knoxville Journal* went as follows:
"World's Fair Motto:
You gouge me and I'll gouge you
And we'll all be broke before we're through."

Dim Bulb

There was one additional story that in all probability was the winning effort in the *News-Sentinel's* short list of Expo investigative stories over the five-year period. Bob Hetherington wrote a very damaging story on May 10, 1981, in which he disclosed that a nonprofit corporation set up by the city to construct an exhibition hall and office building had made certain undocumented payments to the United American Bank.

No follow-up story appeared. This perhaps says as much about the *News-Sentinel's* perspective as any other single item. After waiting a decent length of time for a follow-up, I wrote a letter-to-the-editor in which I stated the following:

> On May 10 the NEWS-SENTINEL carried a story entitled "Roach's Actions Questioned by KEC Directors." The article established the fact that Mayor Tyree and City Law Director Jon Roach, in the name of Knoxville Exhibition Center (a nonprofit corporation set up by the City to build a city-backed exhibition hall and office building on the Expo site) had paid $1.2 million to United American Bank.
>
> The payment to UAB was not documented. That is, no written document was available from either UAB or City officials which explained the transfer of funds.
>
> It is difficult to imagine a story that could cry out more for a follow-up than this one. A large amount of public money is involved; it is being handled by City officials; and what is known about the case offers a rather distinct odor. Yet, aside from a story two days later that essentially did little except restate the issues, the NEWS-SENTINEL, over two months later, has done nothing.
>
> This is public money, Mr. Editor. Doesn't the NEWS-SENTINEL feel any obligation to deal with such issues? Or is this another topic that is too close to Expo and UAB for you to allow your reporters to do their jobs?

Although the letter was not printed, two weeks later on August 7 some additional information appeared buried in a story related to the release of grant funds. This story by Hetherington answered no questions and raised several more. No follow-up occurred.

Organizations frequently try to generate images of their high values with mottoes that find a place over a door or on a letterhead, or in T.V. ads, or some other prominent location for all to see. The *News-Sentinel* offers a double dose. In the upper left-hand corner of the front page conspicuously stands the Scripps-Howard lighthouse, with its light beaming out in all directions. Back on the editorial page we again find the logo but now we have an addition. Beneath the formal title of the paper we find "Ralph L. Millett, Jr. Editor" and "Roger A. Daley Business Manager." And there between Mr. Millett and Mr. Daley and the date we find a thing of beauty: "Give Light and the People Will Find Their Own Way."

Perhaps *Omni's* Dim Bulb Medal had been awarded to the wrong party.

Expo Puff Led the Way

The few *News-Sentinel* stories, the more numerous *Journal* stories, and those of the *Tennessee Journal* were joined by some other quality reporting in the Tennessee area. Janet Breazeale of the *Jackson Sun* (in West Tennessee) did an in-depth story, and Billie Farthing of the *Johnson City Press-Chronicle* (in East Tennessee) did a commendable job on a detailed five-part study of the pros and cons of the exposition. We also knew on a hit-or-miss basis of some elements of the national media that managed to see both sides of the Expo issue. In addition to those already mentioned, specific reference should be made to Joey Ledford, Tom Madden, Steven Holland, and Leon Daniels of United Press International wire service, Bill Osinski of the *Louisville Courier-Journal,* Randy Schultz of the *Post* (West Palm Beach), Kent Biffle of the *Dallas Morning News,* and Wendall Rawls, Jr., of the *New York Times.*

As 1981 progressed the exposition received an increasing degree of attention from papers across the country. Of the coverage 1 saw, Expo puff led the way. But the puffiest of the puffs, and a real coup for Expo's propaganda department and for the *News-Sentinel's* Roger Daley as well, was a two-page, 110 percenter that appeared in *Parade,* the Sunday supplement to a large number of papers across the country, including our own *Knoxville News-Sentinel.* Ironically, in addition to Herbert Kupferberg, who wrote the November 8 story, *Parade's* staff also includes legendary investigative reporter Jack Anderson, whom we had in fact tried to get interested in some of the Expo shenanigans well over two years earlier. Unfortunately, Anderson, who never appears to be at a loss for cases, did not respond to our inquiries.

One cannot help but be reminded of Whittier's famous lines, albeit regarding a different subject:

For of all sad words of tongue or pen,
The saddest are these: "It might have been!"

[In the post-fair period the *Knoxville News-Sentinel* experienced a dramatic increase in its level of performance. Apparently of critical importance was a series of top-level management changes from late 1984 to late 1986. In part, the answer to this improvement may be a commitment to quality by the new personnel. But a big part of the explanation, according to local reporters, is the existence of new people from outside who are not entrenched in the local political and economic elite. The problem which I saw here in chapter 3, the reader will recall, was not the ability of reporters but rather the entrenchment of management into Knoxville's power structure.]

CHAPTER 4
Money Politics

The Heart of the Matter

Enough surely has been said in previous chapters to suggest that quite frequently all was not as it seemed with Expo. Nowhere was this more true than with regard to activity associated with the promoters' key goal: making money. All that has gone before--the sales job, the crushing of a referendum, the media's performance--was related, of course, to money, but here we get a little closer to the dollar itself.

"I have nothing to gain from Expo," said Jake Butcher, Expo chairman, wealthy banker, and two-time candidate for governor. "I only want to do all that I can to see that our state and Southern Appalachia reach their full potential and that all of our people may benefit," Butcher said.

Tomlinson of the *Reader's Digest* saw it somewhat differently. The fair, he said "would be good for Jake Butcher and his friends." The huge project would "channel millions of dollars" through Butcher's United American Bank and "provide fat contracts to business interests" associated with Butcher.

Where do the facts lie? Unfortunately, knowledge of much of the behind-the-scenes activity associated with Expo is hard to come by. The task of getting information is made more difficult when the media is not particularly interested in, maybe even hostile toward, exposing dirty linen.

But, as we saw in the last chapter, all was not darkness. Some scattered information made it into the local press. Other information made it into the out-of-town press. Still more information found its way into federal grant applications. It's not all there by any means, we can assume. But there is enough. A picture emerges of what is at the heart of the World's Fair promotion.

For a glimpse of the direction, the path the money followed and why, one must look closely at both the public and private sectors. Perhaps as good a place as any to start is with the Expo financial consultants.

Who Gets to Play the Game

Someone, of course, had to be a consultant to the Expo Corporation on financial affairs. Someone had to assist in arranging a private loan for the Expo Corporation. Someone had to be on the receiving end of consulting fees that reportedly would be a minimum of $250,000. And so it was that on February 2, 1978, Expo selected Hall-Sledge and Co. as one of two firms to provide financial assistance to the exposition group.

Hall-Sledge in combination with First Boston Corporation, a New York investment banking company, had beaten out what seemed to be potent competitors: Paine Webber; L. F. Rothschild; Lehman Brothers and Kuhn Loeb; and a combined group made up of E. F. Hutton, Goldman-Sachs, and a well-established local firm, Cumberland Securities. Was there a solid reason for the Hall-Sledge victory? It didn't take much to cull an answer from one of the last of Ernie Beazley's 1979 Expo stories.

The *Knoxville Journal* article revealed that Hall-Sledge was only four months old when it was selected. That hardly seemed like a plus. U.S. Securities and Exchange Commission (SEC) records indicated later that the firm's first year of existence hadn't been particularly impressive; it had a net loss of $187,000. Again not much of a plus.

Not established. Not financially prosperous. What then did Hall-Sledge have to warrant its selection over such potent competitors? Beazley's story provides what sounds like the answer. It was composed of the right people.

SEC records revealed that all officers, all directors, and all stockholders (a total of eleven people) had direct links to Jake Butcher's United American Bank. Among the honored were Lionel Wilde, Butcher's brother-in-law, two former UAB vice-presidents who had left UAB to form the firm, major UAB stockholders, and major UAB borrowers.

The Butcher-dominated Expo Corporation merely had done what comes naturally for the Butcher network. The naturalness of the response is reflected in a *Wall Street Journal* article that notes that Butcher didn't "understand all the fuss about his handling of the fair." It then quotes him as saying: "Certainly the people you know, the friends you have in life, are going to enhance a project. But I don't think there's anything been done that shouldn't have been done."

Two groups of people know very well what Butcher means when he says his friends "enhance a project." One group consists of those friends who do the enhancing. But sometimes the enhancing process seems to be rather explicitly at the expense of someone else (that is, aside from taxpayers, who regularly pay for a lot of enhancing). The "someone-else" category is the second group. In the Hall-Sledge case the enhancers and the someone-else group can be easily identified. A somewhat more complex illustration of the enhancing process can be seen in The Hotels Saga.

Let's pick up the story at the January 1979 meeting of the board of directors of Knoxville's Community Development Corporation (KCDC).

(KCDC, as noted earlier, wears two hats. It is the city's public housing authority as well as the city's redevelopment agency. In recent years the redevelopment hat of this so-called independent agency has gotten bigger and bigger. Some students of public administration would say that this change was inevitable. The heyday of public housing expansion was over. Vocal complaints were accelerating from KCDC's public housing tenants. The agency's political power base was slipping. Why not cultivate a new clientele, a new power base, in the world of development? Indeed, how else could bureaucratic expansion occur?)

Landmark of Tennessee was at the meeting in full force--with architect, construction firm, local developer, and a national developer called Landmark Development, Incorporated, out of Minneapolis, Minnesota. Landmark Development looked good. It had recently completed the Notre Dame Complex at South Bend and the Rupp Arena complex at the University of Kentucky in Lexington. Both were class sports arenas with all the trimmings. Landmark was still thinking big: a $25-million complex that would include a 400-room hotel, retail shops, parking for 3,000 cars, and a marina, all of which would be located on a 16-acre tract along with the proposed state pavilion at the south end of the Expo site. With the pavilion scheduled for post-Expo use as a fieldhouse for University of Tennessee basketball games and a convention center, the on-site location adjacent to UT seemed ideal--for the university, for Landmark, for the exposition, and for expanding the tax base, supposedly a basic goal of the Expo project.

The Landmark package was made even more attractive when a Landmark developer said: "We need either Expo '82 or a convention center, but we don't need both."

It did indeed look like Landmark local developer Dan Culp was loaded for bear. But some six months later, Culp was probably thinking that he had been dealing not with a bear, but rather with a weasel. A look at *Webster's Dictionary* would reveal that a weasel is a small and slender animal that is related to the mink and the polecat. "It is very active, bold, and bloodthirsty."

Although Culp's project looked good, Culp himself and the Landmark group didn't fit. Culp had run head-on into the Butcher network in the form of Pegasus Corporation, which included, among others, Butcher's brother-in-law Lionel Wilde. Pegasus was also trying to develop a hotel. And to no one's surprise, Mayor Randy Tyree was there as Pegasus' chief lobbyist and floor-leader.

Outwardly, Knoxvillians were witnessing technical disagreements over the best location for the state pavilion--to the west of the downtown area on the exposition grounds or some one mile away to the east of the downtown area. (At one point there were three different consultants, hired by three different groups, studying the pavilion-location issue. Quite naturally each consultant arrived at the "appropriate" recommendation for his client. You don't pay a consultant good money to tell you what you don't want to hear.) Only slightly submerged was a power struggle between developers with contacts some 200 miles away at the state capitol in Nashville and developers with political power in Knoxville. On one side of the battle was Republican state Senator Victor Ashe, who (with the quiet support of Republican Governor Lamar Alexander's administration) was pushing for the "west" side, a site compatible with Landmark's proposal. Out front on the other side was Mayor Tyree, who knew who was an enhancer and who was not, and therefore demanded use of the "east" side, in the vicinity of the existing coliseum.

The running ordeal of attacks and counterattacks (consultant and counterconsultant) over almost a year ultimately saw three things happen. First, after all the battles were over, no one had won the 1979 War of the Pavilion. The proposed Tennessee state pavilion was dropped for lack of agreement among the powers that be as to where it should be located, and insufficient time to construct it for the exposition, even if agreement could be reached. Second, in due time, the efforts of the Pegasus Corporation led to the development of a franchised Hilton Inn--financed by, developed by, and managed by members of the Butcher network. The Hilton was not located on either the east or the west site, but in between, a block off the exposition grounds. Third, Landmark's 400-room Radisson Hotel was out. The *Tennessee Journal* (August 11, 1980) reported that Landmark proponents said "their project never got off the ground because of lack of cooperation from city and Expo officials." This could be freely translated to read: the proposal was sacrificed on the altar of the Butcher network by the smooth Mayor Tyree in support of hostile Hilton Inn developers.

Tyree had produced a number of solid technical reasons for supporting the east site for a pavilion. As reported by the *News-Sentinel's* Mark McNeely, in a July 1979 article, it would be near the existing civic coliseum with better parking facilities and traffic flow. It had a higher potential for attracting more and larger conventions. The city had made commitments to Hyatt Hotel officials prior to their construction in 1972. Selecting Landmark's west site also might cause the city to lose a federal grant of $5 million. And last but not least, if the state pavilion were built next to Culp's proposed Radisson Hotel, it would constitute "a subsidy for the hotel," said Tyree.

The publicly expressed objections of the Butcher network Hilton Inn developers to Landmark's Radisson were more simple: two hotels was one too many, and the Hilton didn't want competition. "There will not be two hotels built in Knoxville at the same time. It's a fact," said Mack Gentry, a spokesman for the Hilton developers. Gentry also agreed with Tyree that a principle was involved: a pavilion on the west site would be "a subsidy of Landmark." (Watch out for those who wave the flag!)

Two years after the death of Landmark's Radisson Hotel and well before the Hilton Inn was completed, a Holiday Inn Hotel was under construction. "The project closely parallels one proposed by Landmark," the *Tennessee Journal* reported. In fact, the new hotel was on the Expo grounds about a block from the location last mentioned for Landmark's Radisson. It didn't have a state-financed arena but it did have a newly-conceived, city-financed convention facility not just next door, not just attached, but overlapping, with the hotel's bar, pool, lobby, dining rooms, and other such areas within the city's facility and leased from the city, apparently at a considerable savings to the developers. In addition, the hotel was built adjacent to a private parking garage that was financed almost totally by public funds ($6.3 millions of $6.7 million). Is it necessary to point out that the Holiday Inn, unlike the

Culp-Landmark proposed Radisson, was being developed by the "right" people?

Publicly at least, no complaints were heard from the Hilton developers about unfair competition from a second hotel or about a subsidy for a private hotel. Mayor Tyree apparently had forgotten his arguments about east site advantages and principles of free enterprise. But he was there in a familiar role: chief lobbyist and floor leader. For whom? The network works.

Is It Really a Free Enterprise System?

In reality, of course, neither Tyree nor the Hilton developers had any qualms about government assistance to a private project as long as it was the right project. Indeed, the Hilton project itself was a good illustration. To begin with, there was governmental action in acquiring the property under Tennessee's redevelopment law. Value questions were raised about using eminent domain procedures to force one set of property owners to sell their property to the city so that the city could then sell it to another private entity. Whatever happened to the notion of private property, it was asked. The truth is, it's still there-- as long as you have the political clout to keep your property from being declared part of a redevelopment area by city council. But otherwise, an owner seems to be help- less under Tennessee law. Redevelopment, it says, is as le- gitimate a function of local government as construction of a street or a school. Eminent domain applies.

In any case, the Pegasus proposal called for the city, through KCDC, the city's redevelopment agency, to con- demn and acquire the property, sell it to Pegasus, which would in turn develop the hotel and a parking garage. According to initial estimates KCDC would be able to purchase the one-block site for $1.2 million. As usual, the initial estimate was much too low. Ultimately KCDC paid $2 million for the property. It then sold the property to Pegasus for $200,000, which meant a writedown of $1.8 million as an incentive to the developer for doing what most people think ought to be done by developers simply because they are developers. (For the uninitiated, "writedown" is bureaucratese for "gift.") To make the "deal" sound more like a deal, the general public was told by all concerned that although the Hilton would need only 275 parking spaces, the developers would build a 575-space garage, with the extra 300 spaces being available for the public--for parking fees, of course.

So we the public gave the developers $1.8 million and the developers in turn would allow the public to lease parking space. To wonder how such a proposal could be sold is to wonder how politics can be what it is. But sold it was: to the mayor, to the city council, to the KCDC board.

It may sound strange, but apparently the only ones who didn't buy the developers' deal were the developers themselves. They kept the $1.8 million in land, of course, but they thought it would be nice if the city paid for the garage.

When construction started in May 1980, Butcher-network developers, who now included UAB director H. Pat Wood, had managed to make some adjustments. Instead of the Hilton Inn developers financing a 575-space parking garage, the city was financing (and taking the risk for) a 450-space garage and leasing the facility to the Hilton for operation. Moreover, the developers were constructing the parking garage without benefit of competitive bidding. (The available time before Expo made it "unfeasible" to seek bids, city law director Jon Roach told the *News-Sentinel's* Bob Hetherington on March 18, 1980. The garage opened 16 months before the fair did.)

It was a coup for the developers. But how would city taxpayers fare? Although a precise answer cannot be given, the available information does not present a pretty picture.

As of early 1982, all the public financing remains in quietly negotiated short-term notes. But we do have some idea of the city's upfront price tag. On one occasion, the city administration made a proposal for a long-term bond issue to cover land costs and construction of the parking garage. The proposal was later withdrawn, but the issue was to have been for $5.6 million. If bonds could be marketed at 10 percent, which is not the case at present, that would translate into a city payment of some $600,000 a year for a 20-year bond issue.

On the income side, the KCDC-Hilton parking garage lease provides for a yearly payment to the city by the developers of $295,712. As of January 1982 the property taxes on the hotel had not been established. *But,* quite significantly, the lease provides that, if the combined city and county property taxes on the hotel exceed $205,237 at any time during the 26-year life of the lease, then the garage lease payment is reduced by this excess. The result: whatever happens to the city's long-term bond issue, or to the tax rate, or to property-value assessments, the Hilton developers have an iron-clad *maximum* combined annual payment for the garage lease *and* city and county taxes of $500,949 for 26 years. (Hilton has the option to renew the lease for an additional 25 years at the same $295,712 a year, but with no tax credit.)

Most Knoxvillians don't have $1.8 million worth of property presented to them on a silver platter. Most don't have their garages built by the city. Most pay taxes for services, not for payment on their private debts. Most pay more taxes when taxes are increased or reappraisals occur. But then, most Knoxvillians aren't part of the Butcher network.

Perhaps the concerns of Mayor Tyree and the Hilton developers about public subsidies for private projects are now understandable! Who would want to pay taxes to pad someone else's pockets? On the other hand, if they are the *right* pockets . . . Well now, then now. Is it really a free-enterprise system?

[In the post-fair period the Hilton, like other downtown hotels, experienced major financial difficulties. The hotel owners were unable to make their parking garage payments and the city, through KCDC, took possession of the garage in October 1983. In March 1987 the garage was purchased by a private office and hotel group in order to insure parking facilities for the hotel and for a new office complex in an adjoining block. According to the mayor, the selling price of $1.8 million was enough to pay off the remaining debt incurred by the construction of the garage itself (but not the property cost). No provisions have been made for parking by the general public.]

But then again you can't get very far into the reality of the "free enterprise" system, or the "enhancing" system in this case, without turning to the federal government's role. The network didn't end at the city limits.

**The White House and
"How Not to Run the Government"**

Expo contacts with the federal government had their beginnings under the Ford administration; but the real federal commitment came in 1977, in the early days of the Carter administration.

Formal international status as an exposition required the approval of the Bureau of International Exposition (BIE), an international agency located in Paris. To obtain this recognition the Expo people had to have the formal endorsement of the President as well as a commitment for a federal pavilion.

The contacts were in place. Jake Butcher had been an early and substantial contributor to the Carter election drive. He also had established a relationship with chief Carter aide Bert Lance. Butcher's UAB over the previous few months had loaned Lance $433,000. He was borrowing another $130,000 during the period under discussion, according to Tomlinson's *Reader's Digest* article of November 1979. Lance was a good contact. He was not only close to Carter personally, but as director of the Office of Management and Budget he was also in the unique position of guardian of the federal money tree.

The Lance key was turned. Butcher was into the Oval Office almost before President Carter was. By the end of April both the Commerce Department and the President had endorsed Expo. "In the national interest," the President said of the exposition. With his endorsement went an implied commitment to a $20 million federal pavilion. The BIE accepted the President's endorsement. Expo was approved in Washington, in Paris.

But, you may recall, all was not so rosy in Knoxville in 1977. The promoters had a new finance plan (designed to bypass the "masses"), but they could not sell their bonds.

When you can't sell your bonds, what do you do? Why, you apply for a federal grant, of course. And when you run into trouble with the grant, you call on your friends. Unfortunately for the promoters, Bert Lance, who would have been in the key slot, had run into a "peck of trouble" as we say down South, and had gone back to Georgia, with his credibility and his loan portfolio tucked between his legs. But President Carter was still there, and Senator Jim Sasser, whose campaign also had been tied to Butcher money, was still there.

The grant Expo was after was an Urban Development Action Grant (UDAG). The UDAG program in the Department of Housing and Urban Development (HUD) was a new program, put together under the Carter administration. In theory, it was designed to assist "distressed" cities in urban revitalization, with the specific goals of providing jobs for low and moderate income people and a decent environment for housing. The "action" part of the title emphasized that the procedures of application, evaluation, and decision all should occur within one quarter of a year.

The city had put in its $13.8 million UDAG application on January 31, 1978. As indicated in the last chapter, Citizens for a Better Knoxville reacted with a long and detailed analysis of the information provided in the application. Other groups also reacted. Basically the issues were these: citizens had not been informed; public hearings had not been held; and the Knoxville City Council had not approved the application. All were required by law and/or HUD rules. And the city had said they had occurred.

The first quarter ended, and the grant was turned down! Phones rang, trips were made, and meetings were held. Senator Sasser even withheld his support on two crucial Carter-supported amendments to the Panama Canal treaties.

Ultimately, John Means of the *Knoxville Journal* reported on April 15, Sasser saw the President in the Oval Office about Expo money and other Tennessee issues.

"And I told the president," Means quotes Sasser as saying, "that we didn't seem like friends of the administration . . . that we stayed at the end of the line . . . while the squeaky wheels got the grease. . . . And that I was squeaking and would stay squeaking."

At a "shape-up-or-ship-out" cabinet meeting at Camp David, Sasser told Means, his case had been used by the President as a "casebook example of how not to run the government." And the assistant secretaries started calling. Presumably they now knew how to run the government: "What can I do for you, Senator Sasser?"

"I put a shot across his bow," Sasser said.

Presumably Carter, the old Navy man, saw it. According to Anthony Marro's *Washington Star* article of November 1, 1978, Carter sent an inquiry to HUD Secretary Patricia Harris, as to why the UDAG grant had been rejected.

Harris' response contained substantial reasons for the rejection. As Marro reported, "the city had not secured firm commitments for long term use of the property, had not come close to arranging for the needed private investment money, and had not addressed numerous and lengthy citizen complaints about the proposal." Moreover, the chief criterion for selection was "degree of distress," and "out of 300 distressed cities in the nation, Knoxville ranked near the bottom--Number 267."

Carter's reply was brief. In the margin of the Secretary's memo he scribbled: "No need for meeting with me. Just let Tennessee people know about problems and help them comply with requirements."

(Was this the downfall of UDAG as a program that was in fact going to reach its stated goals? Or would the forces of bureaucracy have led it astray anyway? Perhaps the real answer is that Carter's pressure on the UDAG people, along with that of Sasser and other affected members of Congress, simply accelerated the process whereby another program designed to achieve the good, the true, and the beautiful, was sacrificed in the name of political reality.)

The combination of numerous problems with the grant application, the observation of UDAG people that they would not be able to award as much money as the city requested, and Carter's determination to meet the needs of his friends in Tennessee, led the President in June 1978 to push the funding process for Expo up to his Interagency Coordinating Council, located in the White House Office itself. "The President has elevated the Expo '82 project to the high priority level in the White House it deserved," Sasser told UPI. (The President? The White House Office? Expo '82 as a "high level priority" of the U.S. government? Does this tell us something about why major issues, foreign and domestic, seem to explode upon us in the form of crisis, followed by crisis?)

"He (Carter) knows Sasser. He knows Butcher. He felt it was a worthwhile project, so he told us, 'See what you can do for them,'" White House staffer Bruce Kirchenbaum told the *Star's* Marro.

Time passed and "do-for-them" occurred. Although "many of the problems cited by (Secretary) Harris remained," Marro observed, "the funding problem seemed to have been solved."

On October 3 Butcher, who was in the final stages of his gubernatorial campaign, interrupted a swing through the western portion of the state and flew to Washington. The President, flanked by Sasser and Butcher, announced the awarding of $12.45 million in grants to Knoxville for its energy exposition.

"This is not a federal handout," said Carter, as recorded by the *Journal's* John Means in a story on October 4.

"It took your personal attention to get it done," said Butcher.

"It had my personal attention because you and Jim Sasser wouldn't leave me alone," replied Carter.

The timing was good for Expo. The promoters were having trouble putting things together and had to get moving if Expo was going to go. (We have to "leverage the private sector," Kirchenbaum told Marro.) In addition, the Expo opposition back home was getting in a few good licks regarding false claims by the mayor about city council commitments, secret grant applications by the city, and, most of all, by discovering and publicizing a secret finance plan of the mayor and the promoters, whereby they were coming back to the city for a $10 million bond issue. The timing was also supposed to be good for Butcher's campaign.

The timing may have been good, but the smell surrounding the four-agency grant package was not so good. At the time of Carter's announcements, only the UDAG had been evaluated. It had been turned down once, withdrawn just before the awarding hour in the second go-around, and continued to suffer from its earlier maladies.

Another grant in the package had involved the submission of an application to the Economic Development Administration (EDA) in the Department of Commerce, but this application had not been evaluated. No application had been submitted to either the Appalachian Regional Commission (ARC) or to the Department of the Interior, the two other agencies involved in the grant package.

"We simply helped them find federal resources that were available," said Kirchenbaum to Marro.

"Basically, power politics is what it came down to," a Washington source told the *News-Sentinel's* Bob Hetherington.

It is interesting to note that a General Accounting Office (GAO) investigating team looked at the $12.45 million grant process and found nothing illegal. The project has a number of problems, the staff reported, but they are problems at the local level.

In light of all this I feel obligated to take a short break and clearly state, as Charles Peters has so aptly demonstrated in his book *How Washington Really Works,* that the real problems in American politics are not found in abscams and other illegal activities but rather in the everyday workings of the system--in the culture and environment, the workings, of the Presidency, the Congress, the bureaucracy, and in the standard operating procedures of a large portion of state and local governments. It's just the way things are. Do we now have some idea of how the U.S. government can run multi-billion dollar deficits year after year?

Perhaps the point can be driven home more forcibly. On the same day that Carter announced the Knoxville grants, he also announced that he would veto the recently passed public-works bill.

"It's inflationary, it's wasteful, and it spends the taxpayers' money in a very inefficient and inappropriate way. . . . I along with the people of our country are tired of seeing taxpayers' money wasted, and I am determined to see the fight against inflation succeed," the President said.

"The age-old policy of pork barrel allocation is a horrible example to set for the rest of the country," the President had said at a press conference the previous week.

Carter was right. But Carter was wrong. In one breath he had condemned pork barrel allocations and in the next he joined the parade. In the process he had given the Expo promoters the money they needed to shove Expo down our throats.

Carter had literally saved the day for the promoters. Without the federal grants Expo would have been in serious trouble. As mentioned earlier, in order to bypass a referendum on the Expo issue in mid-1977 the promoters had changed their finance plan to one in which KCDC, the city's redevelopment agency, was to sell $46 million in revenue bonds. But the bonds could not be rated. And then Carter came through. The grant package was used as leverage to return the city to its original commitment of $11.66 million.

Needless to say, the promoters argued that things had gone too far for a referendum. Here was free money from the feds. And, of course, there really was no risk for the city. The city, Knoxvillians were assured, would have the 80 acres of land to resell. If it cost $11.66 million, Mayor Randy Tyree kept repeating, we would be able to sell it for just as much. Only a few hardy souls were asking: what about the millions of dollars in improvements that would be purchased, demolished, and carted off to the dump? And a few were saying: you can't buy this property for $11.66 million or anything close to it. You can't relocate the businesses, and especially the railroads, within your budget.

Objections notwithstanding, the pliable city council did its duty. As we have seen earlier, the dodged referendum vote was justified by the sale of short-term, bond-anticipation notes (which would have to be renewed) rather than a long-term bond issue.

In theory the promoters now had a full-blown finance plan. The city's $11.66 million plus the fed's $12.45 million would cover the public component, while a $25 million loan from private banks would provide the private Expo Corporation component. According to the promoters, New York bankers were rushing to join in.

That was in mid-October 1978. In December, after constant urging by the promoters and eventually by the

Commerce Department, President Carter ordered the Secretary of State to issue invitations to the states of the international community. Expo looked oh so good--finally on a firm footing.

But was it? We later discovered that the Commerce Department, even while it was urging the President to issue the invitations, knew that the promoters did not have their financing firmed up. "The issuance of invitations to participate in the exposition at an early date," the Commerce Department's Decision Memorandum of November 29, 1978, said, "would greatly assist the organizers in their efforts to conclude the [private $25 million] credit agreement."

Commerce was trying to leverage the bankers. Someone had to do something. The promoters were still in financial trouble.

Dealing--Downhome and in Washington

The continuing tentativeness of the Expo project became clear with the Beazley run of *Knoxville Journal* articles that began in February 1979. He picked up the cost overruns on property acquisition and relocation costs. It was vociferously denied, but the money just wasn't there. With a string of claims that it was not happening, the site was reduced from 80 to 67 acres. There still was not enough money. With no public acknowledgement, the city, through KCDC, finally concluded that it could not purchase the 67 acres. Eventually, KCDC acquired something less than 30 acres.

Some 37 acres of property belonging to the L&N Railroad and Southern Railroad were left dangling. The promoters, including Mayor Tyree, were reluctant to go back to city council for another bond issue. They had said too many times that the money was there; and even a quiescent people can be awakened, if sufficiently stimulated.

The private Expo Corporation would have to work it out. And what do you do when you have "to work it out"? Why, you go to public bodies.

The choices were obvious. First, there was the University of Tennessee. No problem. It was only a matter of working out the details. Contacts were solid between Butcher and others at the top of the Expo hierarchy and Edward Boling, president of the UT statewide system. As a self-proclaimed member of the "establishment," Boling was more of a businessman than a university president. Moreover, UT under Boling's direction was a highly "developed" institution that was always on the lookout for expansion possibilities. Expo afforded an opportunity not only for cooperation within the Butcher network but also for obtaining land for the university.

A deal was made. For $1 million Expo sold UT 16 acres of Southern's property in the lower portion of the site between Cumberland Avenue and the river. With UT's $1 million, Expo had money to pay Southern's relocation expenses. (Interestingly enough, UT was pleading poor-- relative to support for academic programs, faculty-staff salaries, and existing facilities--before, during, and after the deal. Nevertheless, it managed to whip $1 million out of a contingency fund.)

Expo got use of the land for the exposition; UT got its land for post-Expo use; and Southern retained its main line through the site and perhaps realized a healthy tax write-off for "contributing" its property to the tax-free Expo Corporation.

Everybody got something except the public. This was the area that Landmark initially proposed for its $30 million project. It was the area where the KCDC staff had envisioned for the post-Expo period a private tax-producing research park on the order of that in the Raleigh/Chapel Hill, North Carolina area--with the focus being energy research. The Expo deal took the property out of the tax stream in favor of a surface parking lot for the university. Moreover, the deal left the Southern mainline in place--all the way from one end of the valley to the other. Planning? Redevelopment? Expansion of the tax base? If anyone in Tyree's city administration ever raised an eyebrow, the press missed it.

But the wheeler-dealer approach was far from over. There was the L&N property in the northern part of the site. How could the Expo Corporation come up with the money to deal with it? Perhaps the city could help out.

And so we find that in the very middle of the Expo valley lies 9.2 acres of flood-zone property that the city acquired for $1 million for use as a park in the post-Expo period. Who would use it? How could the city afford to maintain it given the rapidly deteriorating condition of all other parks and public facilities in the city? How would people get to a park surrounded by private property? No such questions were raised. Indeed, essentially nothing was said at the time. It just happened.

The mayor was again the man of the hour. A deal had been swung. Expo got $1 million to deal with the L&N Railroad, free use of the land during the exposition, and the public development of the thirty-inch deep, four-acre Waters of the World. (Some called it Jake's Lake; others, Con Pond.)

(Interestingly enough, at the same time the city was paying $108,695 per acre for this flood-zone property in the valley, it was helping Southern Railroad adjust for its loss of switching facilities by making available an acre of eminently buildable land located not far from the Expo site. For this property, Southern paid the city $8,750.)

But the city commitment still was not enough. There was the remainder of the L&N property, including the old L&N station itself. How could Expo get that land for the duration so that it and the L&N station could be worked into the exposition? The man who was supposed to be getting the answer was Alex Harkness, a former city council member. Reportedly, it was later noted, Harkness had been hired by Expo in April 1979 to put the railroad property into the fold. The UT deal was one component. The city park commitment became the second component. A "private" development was the third.

Harkness first came forth with what was labeled a private development in September 1979. Plans called for a renovation of the L&N station plus construction of a 150,000 square foot office-retail development that could be used by Expo for the Hall of States and Industries during the exposition. It was a $13 million project, with the acquisition and renovation of the station (including some 7 acres of land) costing $3.2 million and the office structure some $9.8 million. Press accounts had Harkness in partnership with John W. McCallie, a local realtor.

Over the next six months the project grew dramatically. By the end of February 1980, its cost was up to $35 million. A hotel and parking garage had been added, and with no explanation the L&N renovation had jumped from a $3.2 million to a $5 million project. A month later, on April Fool's day, Harkness appeared in support of the mayor's appeal to city council for permission to seek a $16 million federal UDAG grant to be worked in as part of a $76.4 million Harkness development project.

Tyree reassured council. "This is a straight grant. The matching money is from private investments, not the city," Tyree said (as quoted by the *News-Sentinel's* Jim Balloch). And look at what we would be getting: $76.4 million in development.

Along the way from $13 million to $76.4 million some interesting information had appeared. Some observers of the Knoxville scene had been suspicious of the real

Harkness role from the beginning. As was later noted in the *Tennessee Journal* (August 11, 1980), Harkness had begun as "a homebuilder in Knoxville and later moved on to small commercial developments." The implied question: was Harkness capable of handling projects of such size?

Some enterprising element of the not-so-loyal opposition among the economically powerful in Knoxville had dug up the partnership certificate by which Harkness' Station Eighty-Two, Ltd. had been established on March 4, 1980. Harkness was there as general partner with a 20 percent interest in the partnership. The McCallie component had slipped badly, with each of four members of the real estate firm holding one percent. Of the other limited partners several were known to have or suspected of having Butcher connections. J. A. Barr, a close Butcher associate, had signed on behalf of James E. McAlexander of Memphis, a major contributor to Butcher's 1978 campaign chest, who had a 20 percent interest. Two other 20 percent shares were held by trustees, one from Knoxville and one from Chattanooga. Trustees for whom? At the April 1, 1980 council meeting Councilwoman Bernice O'Connor tried to find out.

"I don't know who they are and I don't ask who they are. . . . As long as they are investing in our city, why should their names be held up to ridicule?" said Harkness, as recorded by *Journal* reporter Larry Aldridge.

Harkness didn't explain why someone would be held up to ridicule. Could it be because of who was involved?

Four weeks later Harkness himself had slipped. The completed grant application of April 30, 1980, revealed that eight new partnerships had been formed. Station '82 Ltd., with Harkness as general partner, was now dealing only with the L&N Station. Each of the other partnerships had one part of a nine-project package. We now had not only a hotel, an exhibition center, and a parking garage, but also two separate office buildings (one on- and one off-site), two additional parking garages (one on- and one off-site), and a restaurant. It was a grandiose scheme. But who was who, I asked myself as I went through the grant application documents. Each of the partnerships had a general partner and a single limited partner. To me at least, the names had no meaning. All were unknown people with out-of-town addresses.

To fill in all the details concerning the grant application filed by the city with UDAG on April 30, the substantial amendments added on June 25, the rapid approval of the grant by HUD on July 2, and the publicly available information regarding the various additions and alterations that occurred between April and a final contract between HUD and the city in October would be a ponderous task--for me to write; for you to read.

18 USC 1001

But there were some things about developers and about our public officials that are of crucial importance in understanding not only Expo and the Station '82 projects but also our political system--what is done, what isn't done, how it works, how it doesn't work.

One item of particular interest involves a provision at the end of the UDAG grant application. The applicant (in this case, the city through its mayor) "certifies that it has not knowingly and willfully made or used a document or writing containing any false, fictitious, or fraudulent statement or entry." The same provision spells out the penalty for violation: "18 USC (United States Code) 1001 provides that whoever does so within the jurisdiction of any department or agency of the United States shall be fined not more than $10,000 or imprisoned for not more than five years, or both."

In a blistering critique of the original April 30 UDAG application CBK raised a number of questions, some of which seemed to fit into the context of 18 USC 1001. Among other things, we noted that excessive profits were built into the inflated costs of various projects; that other costs had jumped dramatically from earlier estimates; and that Harkness was a handpicked developer of the private Expo Corporation, with nothing vaguely resembling competition in the developer-selection process. We backed up our four pages of concerns with 14 pages of clippings and other information. It was a solid piece of work.

Shortly thereafter, Councilwoman O'Connor decided to go beyond written comments. She and her attorney, Boone Dougherty, made a trip to UDAG offices in Washington in late May. They took me along as part of the local color. Collectively we raised a number of legal issues and reviewed the earlier CBK communications. I tacked on my deep suspicions about the legitimacy of several of the new partnerships.

It would be wrong to say that UDAG officials paid no attention to CBK's critique, or to our personal presentation. Obviously, they forced a number of changes in the original UDAG application. The changes were in an amended version dated June 25, 1980. Among other things, a $9.2 million renovation and expansion of an existing parking garage, the most odorous of the inflated cost projects at perhaps two or more times what it should have been, was dropped from the development package. The L&N Station acquisition and renovation had earlier gone from a $3.2 million to a $5 million project on paper as a private project. When it became part of the original UDAG application, the cost jumped to $7.5 million. In the amendment it was reduced to $5 million.

And there were other changes, the most significant of which was the change in the names of seven of the eight remaining partnerships. Franklin L. Haney had popped up as a general partner for each of the seven partnerships. George W. Ridenour, Jr., was a partner with Haney in four projects and a limited partner in the L&N project. Irby Cooper was a general partner in two others, and James E. McAlexander in the last. Haney was listed as the general contractor for all the projects, including the L&N Station.

Haney is a well-known figure in east Tennessee. He ran in the Democratic primary in the 1974 gubernatorial race (against Butcher, among others). He is a major developer in Chattanooga and in Atlanta and serves as a major supplier of office space for the General Services Administration, the U.S. government agency responsible for providing facilities for U.S. agencies. In addition, he was a prominent supporter of and contributor to Butcher's 1978 gubernatorial campaign.

George W. Ridenour, Jr., is also well known in East Tennessee, although more so in the inner circle than otherwise. He is a member of the firm which serves as legal counsel for Butcher's United American Bank, and is a UAB director. He is generally considered to be a key Butcher aide, as reflected by the fact that he served as chief executive officer of UAB in Butcher's absence during the gubernatorial campaign of 1978.

Irby Cooper and James McAlexander are from Memphis and were major contributors to Butcher's campaign.

Equally as important as those who appeared as partners are those who disappeared. In reviewing the UDAG application in April, I had noticed the large number of Chattanooga addresses, the lack of public visibility of people who in some instances were supposedly putting up millions of dollars in cash equity, and, most suspicious of all, the fact that the dominant equity role in five of the eight new partnerships was played by women.

"I don't know much about the world of high finance, but I do know that it isn't dominated by women," I told *Knoxville Journal* editor Bill Childress.

Some three months after I had made this observation to the *Journal* and six weeks after the switch to Haney, Ridenour, and the others had actually occurred, the *Tennessee Journal* on August 11 and the *Knoxville Journal* on August 12 and 13 disclosed that those who originally appeared as partners had not been drawn at random. Beazley of the *Knoxville Journal* observed that at least 10 of the 16 partners "are tied to Haney." The relationships ranged from jobs as Haney's secretary and chauffeur to relatives and business associates. Of the remaining six, three had given Chattanooga area addresses and two others had offices in Butcher's UAB office building. The sixth appeared in a picture on a Knoxville society page in 1981. He was attending a function at Jake Butcher's Whirlwind home along with Bert Lance and other Democrats from the region.

Did the partnerships indicate violations of 18 USC 1001? Did these documents contain "false, fictitious or fraudulent" statements? Beazley's coverage of Harkness' explanation for the fronts is suggestive.

"Harkness also said their decision to list friends, employees, and relatives of Haney as partners in the project was principally a procedural ploy to obtain tax-exempt industrial bond financing and federal funds until they found investors for the project." Beazley quoted Harkness as stating: "At the time, we frankly did not know who was going to put up the equity in the buildings. . . . The partners were to be listed temporarily until the actual investors were put in place."

Beazley, and the *Tennessee Journal* to a lesser extent, also disclosed that the connections to the Butcher network were even more firm than suggested by the Haney-Ridenour roles. The brains behind the financing for the complex project had been Jesse Barr, a longtime Butcher confidant with an office in Butcher's executive suite in UAB Plaza. According to Harkness, Barr was brought in because of his financial talents. Beazley quoted Harkness: "I know of his ability and have known of his ability for years. . . . He's one of the sharpest people in the financial field in the South."

Barr attracted substantial attention in both the *Tennessee Journal* and the *Knoxville Journal* news accounts as a result of his earlier career with Union Planters National Bank of Memphis. He had left the bank in

January 1975. Later that year he was charged in two federal indictments. Beazley observed that Barr was convicted on September 30, 1976, on "25 of 31 federal counts of bank fraud ranging from embezzlement to misapplication and conversion of nearly $17 million of Union Planters Bank funds to his own personal use, mainly speculative real estate development." He served about one year of a five-year sentence at the federal minimum security prison at Elgin Air Force Base in Florida.

As a result of his conviction Barr, under U.S. banking regulations, could never again legally be an employee of a bank. Beazley stated that UAB insisted that Barr was only a consultant, but "other evidence suggests that he is actively representing the bank's interest in the exposition as a whole" as well as in the Station '82 developments. The evidence seemed firm. On at least some crucial issues, Barr spoke for Butcher.

The amended eight-project, (now) $67 million package obviously had a Butcher network cast of characters. Moreover, federal government documents also revealed that the developer equity for six of the projects was covered by UAB letters of credit. The bond sales on one project were secured by a UAB letter of credit. All told, UAB letters of credit came to $9.9 million. Except for $3.1 million from other private sources, all the remaining money involved public funds and tax-free industrial development bonds.

Due to the efforts of CBK, UDAG officials in HUD knew about the fronts and about other false and misleading aspects of the application. The HUD Inspector General's Office had the information. [As will be seen in Book Two, the HUD Inspector General's Office sharply criticized the administration of the UDAG grant in a 1983 post-fair audit.] The Federal Bureau of Investigation (FBI) was also aware of the situation. Apparently, the FBI pursued the matter far enough to have its investigation terminated by John Cary, the U.S. Attorney for East Tennessee.

(The U.S. Attorney is the prosecuting arm of the federal government. This position remains as one of the two key patronage plums--the other being that of federal judge--to be given out by U.S. Senators of the President's political party. Although these appointments technically are made by the President, the appointment in the present case presumably was actually in the hands of Democratic Senator James Sasser. Sasser had pushed for UDAG approval, had been a prime supporter of Expo at the federal level, and had close connections to Butcher. It is not known whether such factors either directly or indirectly influenced the decision of U.S. Attorney Cary. Be that as it may, a number of earlier cases indicate that the U.S. Attorney selection process is a hell-of-a-way to run the system, if even the appearance of an unbiased administration of criminal justice is desired. An excellent illustration occurred in the 1977-78 Marston affair. The Carter administration, at the urging of Democratic U.S. Representative Joshua Eilberg, fired Philadelphia U.S. Attorney David Marston, who at the time just happened to be investigating none other than Representative Eilberg himself. Marston "doesn't do anything but prosecute Democrats," Eilberg had told the President, according to a *New York Times Magazine* article by William Safire. On the other hand, Marston is quoted by the *U.S. News & World Report* of February 6, 1978, as stating that "no amount of rhetoric will ever convince the bagmen and the fixers that they can't pull strings in Washington, because they're sure that strings got pulled in Washington." The same *U.S. News* article noted that the Marston affair led Carter's Attorney General Griffin Bell to require all U.S. Attorneys to notify the Justice Department "in writing when investigating public figures.")

Given the circumstances, it came as no surprise when an FBI agent informed me that they had to watch out for the "sensitive" political cases. And watch out they did. All investigations came to the same conclusion concerning the questionable aspects of the UDAG application: "It's accepted practice." That's also a hell-of-a-way to run a system.

More Public Money, No Competitive Bidding

In due time the UDAG grant process started to wind down. Substantial changes, however, continued to occur even after the amendments of June 25. Indeed, change after change led to a financial scheme so complex as to defy simple description.

One of the most important changes was the disappearance of two of the private partnerships, which were to have built an on-site office building and an on-site exhibition hall. They were replaced by Knoxville Exhibition Center, Inc. (KEC), a non-profit corporation established by the city to build a combined office and exhibition structure called Knoxville Exhibition Center. Financially, the office/exhibition building was supported totally and unconditionally by the city taxpayers through a KEC-city lease agreement that called for city operation of the two facilities. The city's obligation was a minimum of $1.9 million a year over 30 years, the equivalent of the debt payment on a $21 million bond issue.

Another nonprofit corporation, Knoxville Civic Revitalization Fund (KCRF), was established by the city to hand out $14.5 million in public money, $9.9 million of which came from the UDAG grant, and $4.6 million of which came from the Expo Corporation as payment for use of the city-financed KEC exhibition hall and office building during the exposition. The $4.6 million was *given* outright by KCRF in varying amounts to four of the private partnerships. The $9.9 million from the UDAG was "loaned" to the same four privately owned projects at below market rates (eight percent collectively). This obviously was a very special kind of "loan." The private partnerships were required to make yearly "interest-only" payments with no payment, *ever*, of the principal. Try to get your friendly banker to agree to this kind of "loan." But then your friendly banker is not the City of Knoxville or Uncle Sam. And, of course, you are unlikely to be a part of the Butcher network.

Those to whom Santa Claus paid a visit were the L&N Station--$4.1 million of its total cost of $5 million was obtained from KCRF public money; Sunsphere Restaurant--$1 million of its total cost of $5.2 million; Holiday Inn Parking Garage--$6.3 million of its total cost of $6.7 million; Summit Hill Parking Garage--$3.1 million of its total cost of $3.5 million. [This garage was not built.]

In theory these four projects collectively were to make "interest-only" payments of $800,000 a year for 30 years to the KCRF trust, which would turn the money over to KEC to assist the city in meeting its $1.9 million a year obligation. Significantly, however, the partnerships' own "Cash Flow after Debt Services" statements, as found in the UDAG application, reveal a set of projects that are far from formidable financial operations, thereby raising questions as to whether they will be able to meet the $800,000 payment. More secure was another $200,000 to be received by KCRF, and applied to the city's commitment, from a lease to the Holiday Inn of space within the exhibition center and the office building.

The remainder of the city's obligation was to be met by income received from the operation of the exhibition hall and the office building, neither of which had been subjected to a meaningful economic feasibility analysis. Since the exhibition hall was not expected to do more than cover its operational expenses, the entirety of the remaining $900,000 obligation rested on the ability of the city to profitably lease its office building.

Initially, the city's line regarding the profitability of the office building was a simple one. It'll be no problem, said the mayor in an offhand manner. But city operations officer Bill Ricker was forced to admit, under oath in a court case, that the city had calculated a $360,000 a year loss on the combined operation of the two city-financed facilities. (The court case involved a challenge by Councilwoman O'Connor of the constitutionality of the eight-project package under the Tennessee constitution, which prohibits a local government from loaning its credit to a private entity without first obtaining approval of its people via a referendum. Apparently these words have no meaning. She lost.)

Even Ricker's under-oath $360,000 estimate is open to serious question in view of the city's past record of best-of-all-worlds' answers. A more realistic expectation of the combined operation of the exhibition hall and the office building, once operational expenses as well as debt service are considered, is a yearly loss of some $900,000, assuming that the private partnerships in fact kick in their $800,000 interest payment.

[As will be seen in Book Two, I was far too optimistic concerning the city's loss. As of mid-1987 only one of the projects was current in its loan payments, and the Holiday Inn was behind in its lease payments. Moreover, the convention center has operated (even without considering depreciation) at a loss every year since the fair, with the most recent figure available (1986) showing red ink of over $230,000. The only positive development was the 1987 sale of the city's office building to the state for $4.7 million. Even so, the city's loss appears to be a minimum of some $1 million a year over Ricker's $360,000 estimate.]

Under the circumstances, it might legitimately be asked why the city was constructing an office building, particularly since it had just moved into a new $33 million facility. As incredible as it may seem, no answer was forthcoming. This leaves one to speculate that it was built so that it could be built--by someone, for money.

Significantly, no competitive bidding occurred on this or any of the other projects of the Station '82 development, even though a number of them involved large quantities of public money. City officials seemed especially interested in having it that way with respect to the totally city-financed exhibition hall/office building complex. Why? Was it because competitive bidding might not lead to the right people coming up with the right figures?

As it turned out, the figures that did emerge appeared to be grossly inflated in several instances. CBK's initial contact with UDAG officials regarding the April 30, 1980, grant application pointed out that on the basis of comparable costs of other buildings in the area several of the UDAG projects seemed to have multimillion dollar "slack" in them. Among those noted was the city-backed office building. The *Tennessee Journal* (April 20, 1981) later observed that the cost per square foot of the office building "is almost twice as much as the . . . per square foot figure quoted for the new Cedar Bluff office building in Knoxville, which one developer described as the finest of its kind, 'a real Cadillac of a building.'"

The projected cost of the Holiday Inn parking garage also seemed to be inflated. Only two blocks away from this 420-space, $6.7 million structure (with $6.3 million of its cost covered by public money) stands the slightly larger Hilton Hotel parking garage, which cost less than $2.5 million. The *Tennessee Journal* (August 11, 1980) observed, when the Holiday Inn garage was scheduled to be one hundred parking spaces larger than it actually turned out to be, that builders said the cost per parking space was "more than double the average cost." A satisfactory explanation of the apparently unusually high costs was never given.

Presumably such inflated costs would not have occurred with an open-bidding process, but as we have seen, openness was not characteristic of the Station '82 development. In spite of the fact that it involved huge sums of public money as well as use of the power of eminent domain, the entire development had been closed.

The developers had been handpicked by the Expo-UAB team with the city and HUD simply acquiescing. We had seen the Butcher network in operation. The principle is the principal. That's the way it is in money politics.

CHAPTER 5
All's Not Fair

Expo was deceit. Expo was hypocrisy. Expo was a blitz that bypassed the people. Expo was manipulation of the press. And Expo was money.

"It's a hell of a depressing situation down here," I told the *Washington Star's* Anthony Marro in October 1978. It got worse, and it wasn't just "down here."

The United States government constructed a pavilion for a World's Fair with the theme of energy. The $12.4 million structure was not energy efficient. Expo was energy, American style.

The city government, without benefit of competitive bidding, constructed an exhibition hall and an office building that could be used, according to the developer, "for whatever the city wants to use them for." Expo was planning, American style.

A privately owned parking garage was constructed at what appeared to be grossly inflated costs, with the bulk of the price being borne by the public. Expo was development, American style.

But when all was said and done, Expo most of all was politics, American style.

Down here in Knoxville, the evidence suggests, the leading lights, both in and out of government, are primarily, if not exclusively, interested in what comes out of the system--not how it is done, not who does it, but what is done for whom. "The people of Knoxville and the people who will go to the fair are of almost no importance. The real stakes, the real high stakes, are much more long term and involve the people who really have the power," a Knoxville attorney told Randy Schultz of the West Palm Beach *Post*.

The promoters owned Knoxville.

And through the efforts of wealthy banker Jake Butcher, they carved out a piece of the White House under Jimmy Carter. From Carter and Senator Jim Sasser they obtained a piece of the bureaucracy--and its money, and more of its money.

When Ronald Reagan became President in January 1981 the promoters managed the transition in grand style, primarily through their link to Republican Senator Howard Baker. Baker had been there all along but had maintained a low profile. Robert Worthington, a Baker friend and law-firm partner, was the Expo legal counsel and the apparent contact.

When Baker became the majority leader in the Republican-controlled U.S. Senate, he was crucial not only as a contact with the Reagan administration and its grants but also as a boost for the sagging Expo performance in signing up corporate exhibitors. Baker firmly embraced the project, held a dinner for corporate executives at which he urged them to participate in Expo, and stimulated Secretary of State Alexander Haig's interest in encouraging international participation.

The promoters--Democrat and Republican, Butcher and all--needed Baker. Presumably, Baker saw an opportunity not only to aid some friends but also, through Expo exposure, to fan the sparks of support for his continuing presidential ambitions. Republican Governor Lamar Alexander followed Baker's lead, perhaps for the same reason. "At bedrock," said Randy Schultz, "no political differences divide men who see mutual benefit in a venture." Expo surely was politics, American style.

Washington, says Charles Peters, is a make believe world. "In Washington bureaucrats confer, the president proclaims, and the Congress legislates, but the impact on reality is negligible if evident at all. The nation's problems don't disappear, and all the activity that supposedly was dedicated to their solution turns out to be make believe."

Congressmen legislate, pretend, allocate money--and get re-elected. Bureaucrats execute, pretend, spend money-- and maintain and expand. Special interests request, pretend, obtain money--and get rich. And the nation's problems endure.

But such amoral rot is not something found only in Washington. More and more for the local political and economic elite, neither the particular program nor its purpose is of any consequence. "If it's for money, I'm for it."

And they regard it as free money.

"It won't cost the taxpayers a cent. We are applying for a federal grant," said Mayor Tyree in regard to a proposed mile-long $13 million monorail "people-mover" that would serve essentially no purpose after the exposition. With the necessary adjustment, similar statements are being made all over the country. And those who administer the programs and those who are the chief beneficiaries (the politicians, bankers, developers, consultants, et cetera, et cetera, et cetera) have little, if any, sense of responsibility to the ultimate source of the funds--the taxpaying general public. Nor is there any sense of remorse when the professed goals of program after program are sabotaged by their actions.

"Unfortunately, the spending floodgates, once opened, are manipulated to permit a diversion of much of the public money to help those who don't need it," said Senator William Proxmire in his *The Fleecing of American.* "The poor run interference, the well-to-do score the touchdowns." The UDAG program is a case in point, he said, "with the poor neighborhoods picking up a few scraps."

"Congress does not make policy; it simply distributes . . . the pork," wrote David Stockman in his 1975 "Social Pork Barrel" article. Only by looking at middle- and upper-class "welfare," he stated, can we explain the expenditure of billions of dollars and the continued existence of "25 million poor Americans in a $1.5 trillion economy." Indeed, as Morris Fiorina so aptly observed in his book entitled *Congress,* "the general, long-term welfare of the United States is no more than an incidental by-product of the system."

The picture is not a pretty one as we march on through the last quarter of the twentieth century, all the while experiencing runaway budgetary deficits, skyrocketing inflation, high unemployment, and other social problems that won't go away. But what happens in Washington and in the Knoxvilles of this country does not have to happen. Reform is called for. Reform is possible.

People need to know the system, how it works, and how it does not work. Reform is education.

People need to think beyond their own personal gain to the welfare of the society as a whole. Reform is morality.

People need to act to break the institutional imperatives of Congress, of the Presidency, of the bureaucracy, of the special interests. Reform is democracy.

Book II

The World's Fair and After

INTRODUCTION, 1987

In early 1987 as the author began agonizing over
what should now be written about the Knoxville World's
Fair and its aftermath, Book One of this study was over
five years old. Newspaper clippings had accumulated--by
the boxful. Scattered handwritten notes with numerous
ideas had been jotted down and set aside. The five-plus
years had been crammed with facts. Nor was all the information merely an accumulation of dry facts; the human
stories were reflective of Dickens--the best of times, the
worst of times.

The fair did open on schedule. It ran its six month
course with a high degree of organizational efficiency.
The ups were there. And so were the downs. Basically, the
fair as an entertainment event was fairly well received,
with most of the visitors enjoying themselves. Knoxville
International Energy Exposition (KIEE), the Expo
Corporation, said it reached the projected attendance of 11
million visits. It was able, KIEE reported, to pay off an
up-front $33 million loan and end up in the black.

But the fair's impact on Knoxville's economy was far
more mixed. To be sure, the times were good for many. On
the site itself, activity was brisk with near perfect weather
over the six months. Rides were taken; beer was consumed;
Petros were eaten. To the chagrin of many others,
however, the fair was a world class bust. In spite of wide-
spread expectations to the contrary, the fair was played
out largely on-site with off-site economic activities dramatically less than expected. "Everyone was going to get
rich and live forever," wrote *Knoxville Journal* columnist
Jim Dykes. "But the tour buses screwed up everybody
except their riders." In the first four months of 1983 the
number of bankruptcy petitions jumped 15 percent over
the corresponding period in 1982. One of the big reasons:
World's Fair dreams that didn't come true.

As the fair closed its gates on October 31, 1982,
board chairman Jake Butcher was riding high. He was also
riding high four blocks away at his United American Bank
(UAB).

Two years later almost to the day, Jake Butcher was
being indicted in the United States District Court in
Knoxville on criminal charges stemming from the
operations of his banks in Knoxville and Chattanooga.

111

"It was a grim day for Butcher," wrote *Nashville Tennessean* reporters Larry Daughtrey and James Pratt. Knoxville's "symbol of wealth, power, and glamour," they said, had been "portrayed by federal prosecutors . . . as an uncommon thief who used forged signatures and fictitious companies to drain millions of depositors' dollars into his own bank accounts."

Two blocks up Main Avenue from the U.S. District Court stood the glimmering 27-story glass office tower in which many of Butcher's exploits had taken place. But Knoxville's dominant downtown landmark no longer housed UAB, formerly Knoxville's largest bank and the flagship of Butcher's five-bank $1.5 billion empire. Jake Butcher's banking empire, as well as a 22-bank $1.5 billion system controlled by brother C. H. Butcher, Jr., had toppled, victims of banking practices that defy the imagination.

Jake Butcher, however, did continue to have a presence in the old UAB Plaza, now renamed the Plaza Tower. Located on the fifteenth floor is the U.S. Bankruptcy Court, which contained the bulging bankruptcy files of Jake Butcher, C. H. Butcher, Jr., several of their relatives, and a number of former business associates. The *Knoxville News-Sentinel* reported in early 1985 that the "number of bankruptcies related to the Butcher bank failure exceeded 200." For Jake and his friends, it was a downer. And it got worse.

One block out Main in the other direction from the U.S. Court House lay the site of the Butcher-dominated 1982 World's Fair. Unlike the explosive experiences of Jake Butcher and his banks during the two years after the fair closed, the old World's Fair site had been strangely silent. Indeed, for those who had experienced the bustling humanity of the fair during its six month's run from May 1 to October 31, 1982, the site might have produced a slight case of culture shock if viewed in the fall of 1984.

To be sure, familiar scenes were there.

The Sunsphere still rose tall from the Lower Second Creek valley floor. Atop the 266 foot "theme structure" of the fair the gold-tinted glass ball still sparkled in the sun, just as it had done when thousands of people walked in its shadow daily, while hundreds of others stood in line for $2 elevator rides to the top and a chance to sample "world class" food in the Sunsphere Restaurant.

But things had changed. The elevator was shut down in 1984. No restaurant. No people. No money. It was just there. By mid-1987, it was again in use. But not as a world class restaurant or night club, as some had proposed, but rather as the home of the local Arts Council, with the city now owning the building, collecting no taxes, leasing it for $1 a year, and paying for the utilities.

No one spells it out, but perhaps the Sunsphere still suggests the dominant theme of the fair site. This time around though, the Sunsphere reflects not the festive atmosphere of the fair itself but rather what came after the fair closed in October 1982, what came in the way of fair site redevelopment. Things went downhill, bottomed out, and then edged up, but not much, and time passed, with much expressed hope, and more city money.

CHAPTER 6
Some Fair, Some Foul

"All the Ships Will Rise"

Surely bankruptcy and ultimately city ownership for the World's Fair theme structure weren't the expectation when the idea of an international exposition was first introduced in 1976. The reader will recall that the promoters' promises for the Knoxville community for the long-run future were nothing but glow and grow.

A state pavilion would be built. After the fair it would become a new convention center for the city and an arena for University of Tennessee basketball. The U.S. Pavilion would be another big-bucks building that would be used for the United States fair program and then become a high-powered energy research center in the post-fair period. The deteriorating inner-city neighborhoods would be resurrected. Downtown retail sales would double. Jobs would be created. The fair would produce an elevated people mover, a lake marina, railroad connections to Gatlinburg, everything, including super planing. That November 1976 pamphlet said it all: Expo "will provide an opportunity for fifty years of positive and progressive growth in a five-year span."

"When the tide comes in, all the ships will rise," said fair board chairman Jake Butcher.

Knoxville was on a roll. Soon it would be a city with super services, an expanded tax base, a united and wealthy people, and worldwide recognition as the energy capitol of the world. And, said the promoters, it would all occur at no cost, no risk for Knoxville or its taxpayers.

The glow did have some reality to it both before and during the fair. As the reader will recall from Book One, improvements to the interstate system were accelerated. Some private cleanups also occurred. The site itself was cleared of unused railroad tracks, dilapidated houses and warehouses. Economic development did occur and jobs were created as better than $80 million in public money and perhaps half as much in private money was pumped into the fair site and the surrounding area. Large-scale multi-million dollar projects were undertaken, as were small projects by more or less ordinary folks who saw dollars in the tourist influx.

115

The Polyester Ladies Got Petrofied

When the 1982 World's Fair opened on May 1, 1982, the people did come. And while all was not rosy, the fair in many respects was a successful one.

"We fell in love with your area," wrote Bernard and Pat Mazenac of Bozeman, Montana, in a November 1982 letter to the *News-Sentinel*. "Everyone at the Fair was so courteous and we enjoyed every minute of it." The Mazanecs were so impressed that Bernard was seeking a Knoxville position as an architect, "hoping that someday soon we will be able to call Knoxville our home town."

In a first anniversary editorial the UT student newspaper pointed to the positive: summer jobs; new friends, some from other countries; "fascinating cultural events"; "honored guests" such as President Reagan and former President Carter; "renovation" of "dilapidated areas." The *Daily Beacon* also noted that the fair produced a "renewed pride in our city" and "put Knoxville on the map."

But the fair for some was more than the mere ticking off of the positives. On the occasion of the first anniversary of the fair's opening, 63 year old Mondilee Buckner said to a *Knoxville Journal* reporter: "I wish it was like last year. I cried when it left."

And then we find the recollections of *Knoxville Journal* columnist Jim Dykes in a fifth anniversary article. Jim, as he reports it, was there on opening day and was refused admission to the Baptist Pavilion "on the specious grounds" that he was drunk. It went uphill from there:

> After my rejection by the Baptists, I figure I was going to hell anyway, so I might as well dance. And dance I did. Bunnyhopping all around the Strohaus to the beat of an oompah band, clinking beer steins with total strangers, waltzing on table tops with little, round, middle-aged ladies from Toledo and Akron, who wore doubleknit polyester pantsuits (blue and pink, to match their hair). When the polyester ladies had a good time, everybody had a good time.
>
> After the Fair, we all wondered what had happened to the cozy ambiance of the Strohaus. We had never before known that that many people could get together to dance and drink beer without somebody getting cut

or shot. We finally figured out that it was the little round polyester ladies who made the difference. They were as irresistibly happy and innocent as so many Labrador puppies.

Like another famous beer promoter Jim too has trouble getting respect. So let's note that if Jim says the little round polyester ladies had a good time, they had a good time, I suppose.

But happy or no, they brought their money. All told, KIEE said, the fair organization took in and then paid out some $114 million. On the fair ground otherwise, additional money was spent on amusement rides, food and drink, and souvenirs.

Surely the golden story of the small-scale entrepreneurs was that of Joe Schoentrup. Joe borrowed an idea from Dallas Dairy Queens, "put the gourmet in it," left his job in Spokane, came to Knoxville with his two-women, two-men operation, and sold his Petros. Perhaps the most widely-known food product of the fair, the Petro is a small bag of Fritos with the top cut off and layers of chili, shredded cheese, chopped scallions, chopped tomatoes, sour cream, and hot sauce added on the corn chips in the bag itself.

"We had a captive audience," Joe said in a June 1987 interview, and we "got them Petrofied." Asked about the present, Joe observed that "yes, we're still doing the bag," with one franchise outlet in Knoxville and his own operation in Spokane. He expects another unit in each city in the near future. "Our goal," he said, "is the Petrofication of America, but we're a little behind. It's different out in the real world."

But, he said, the Knoxville fair was "wonderful for us." And, he added, the other concessionaires also did well, "some much better than we did."

The dollars also flowed to certain establishments outside the fair fence. Some of the hotels and motels boomed during the fair. Some of the restaurants prospered.

Thus viewed, the pre-fair and fair times did have a positive side. But the fair also had warts--lots of them, going all the way back to the beginning.

Jake's Fair

The central focus of Book One was those warts, as seen in the time period from early 1977 to early 1982: promises made, many already unkept; referendum movement undone; media prostitution; money directed.

Several component parts of these topics will unfold further as this study continues. But two items were breaking even as *Exposé* went to press in early 1982.

The chapter dealing with "money politics" has already pointed to a directional flow in the expenditure of both private and public funds. Jake Butcher's friends and associates seemed to be in the right place at the right time, or so they assumed. The case became even more solid in April 1982, when *Chicago Tribune* writers James Coates and Andy Knott looked at the 1982 World's Fair building permits and other information and concluded in a 75-column-inch story that "behind Jake's Fair is a story of how millions of tax dollars were spent without competitive bidding . . ., how a small group of the South's power brokers awarded each other business deals in fair related projects."

Several of the participants involved in such deals were interviewed by Coates and Knott. They "all insisted," the writers noted, that "there was no conflict of interest and said that their involvements were only due to pursuit of free enterprise."

"The story," Butcher said in a letter to *Chicago Tribune* editor James Squires (as carried in the *News-Sentinel* of April 16), "conveys a transparently false picture," and has "tainted leading businessmen of our city, the politicians of our region, and the American entrepreneurial spirit that has breathed life into our Fair." No retraction, no apology, appeared in the *Tribune*.

One man's "American entrepreneurial spirit," of course, may be something quite different for another man. The reader may recall from Book One the words of that disenchanted contractor who was cut out of the hotel action by Butcher and his associates: "Some people around here just have to operate under the pig theory."

In any case, Coates and Knott apparently pulled Butcher's chain one link too many. Jake, one of the reporters said later, had flown off to Chicago in an attempt to have the reporters fired. Coates and Knott survived to cover the UAB collapse.

Wheeling and dealing with money is surely one of the more important political aspects of the Expo case. Little doubt would exist over the most important of the human aspects: here we find the eviction of people from their apartments, their trailer courts, their rented homes. With world class levels of publicity about millions of people expected for the fair, about too few motel rooms, about dramatic increases in motel and campground rates, wasn't there room for money to be made?

In a special story in the *Wall Street Journal* of February 19, 1982, Ernie Beazley wrote that "about a thousand tenants, some elderly and handicapped, were getting evicted by landlords scrambling to offer housing at inflated rates for visitors to the 1982 World's Fair." Other owners were more subtle than simply engaging in direct evictions. Beazley reported that one landlord had raised rents $100 a month in order to create vacancies. He expected the apartments to rent for $144 a day during the fair. When asked about the propriety of such action, he indicated that it wasn't done lightly. "I'm a Christian, and I prayed before I did this," he said. It's called "Gouging for Christ," editorialized *The Christian Century* in March 1982.

The pre-fair period surely did have its negatives and its bad images. Just as surely, the fair wasn't all glow for some of the visitors. Certainly it didn't play well for Carrick H. Patterson, a reporter for the *Arkansas Gazette*. Patterson attended the fair with a group of children and parents from her daughter's school. Her extended May 30, 1982, story was a roast. Good things were present, she said: the cleanliness, the cheerful employees, the fireworks, the Chinese and Peruvian pavilions, stood out. But the fair had too little of fun, educational value and foreign culture, too much of "boring exhibits, long lines and high prices." The story's lead catches the general drift: "With the 1982 World's Fair in neighboring Tennessee, many Arkansans have thought they'd pack up the kids this summer and give it a visit. Many will wish they hadn't."

It's a long way from Little Rock to New York but images don't necessarily change. No less critical were two early May articles by noted New York *Daily News* critic Rex Reed. Reed wasn't all rip: The world's largest miniature circus, "handmade to one-sixteenth the size of the early Ringling Bros. and Barnum and Bailey Circuses, . . . will delight kids of all ages." On the other hand, Reed wrote, if you had been to the 1964 New York World's Fair with its bizarre buildings, exotic foods, magnificent shows, and extravagant corporate pavilions, you simply had to see Knoxville's fair as a "modest event." "If they held a fair like this one in the heart of New York City, Rex said, "nobody would come."

And it wasn't just visiting reporters sand critics who had trouble with the fair. Shortly after the fair opened UPI carried the experiences of the Michael Sharp family from Holly, Michigan. The Sharps, UPI reported, stayed at a $75 a night motel arranged by Knoxvisit, one of the reservation services. Mrs. Sharp expected a resort hotel, but "it truly was a dump," she said. And then there were the lines and the prices at the fair itself.

The Sharps skipped their second day at the fair, even though they had tickets. "We're never coming back here. These people are greedy. This is just one big ripoff," said Mrs. Sharp.

A Slippery Gangplank

Most Knoxvillians, of course, were not part of the ripoff parade in any sense. But even for those who jumped head first into the tourist industry, was it greed or presumed opportunity seized? If all the ships are going to rise, said both the hustler and the legitimate entrepreneur, I'm getting on board. But as the fair opened and the tourists arrived many discovered that the ship had a slippery gangplank.

The evidence piled up almost immediately. The 1982 World's Fair was occurring largely within the gates of the fair, with only limited economic impact off the site itself. One night, said Jim Dykes in that May 1, 1987, *Journal* story, "I went to the Hyatt where a seven-piece band was playing to a three-piece audience."

Many well-established enterprises such as restaurants, theaters, record shops, and clothing stores, some only a short distance from the fair, actually lost business. "We had a rough time because of the Fair," said Michael Rhea, manager of the Knoxville Dinner Theatre. The fair, he told the *Knoxville Journal,* "took all the entertainment money in town." Larry Duby, planning director for the Knoxville Zoo concurred. "The fair damn near killed us," he said in an April 1985 interview.

Economic enterprises directly associated with the fair's presence frequently suffered a similar fate. Off-site, fair sponsored entertainment events at the Civic Coliseum and the Tennessee Theater were cancelled by the number. The operators of parking lots, trinket shops, bus lines, campgrounds, trailer parks, and supplemental housing units sharply curtailed or ceased their activities entirely.

The story of one such ill-fated business was told by Fred Brown of the *News-Sentinel* in a September 1984 feature story. Leonard Shields, Brown said, had been anticipating. "World's Fair tourists were going to be arriving like locusts. Everyone said so. Shields wanted to be ready for the stampede." For Shields, Brown observed, the fair "was the chance of several lifetimes." So he quit his job as a long-distance truck driver and borrowed the money to build "Hillbilly Haven," complete with all the trimmings, including a goat-cart ride. Brown quotes Shields: "If the tourists wanted to see hillbillies, I was going to give it to 'em."

Hillbilly Haven was a bust. The tourists didn't come but the loan payment notices did. And Shield's dream, like those of so many others, is gone.

"You know," he said to Brown, "I started out with a lot. Now I don't even have a job."

Fred Ramos also had a touch of World's Fair fever as 1982 approached, but he didn't expect to make a mint when he bought and fixed up a four-apartment Victorian house located about two miles from the fair site. "About $60,000, that's what I thought I would get altogether," he said in a February 1985 interview. "They showed me the reservations and the figures," he said of agents from World Property Management (WPM), and one of the fair's three housing reservation services.

Asked how much he had made, Ramos replied simply: "Nothing." The money went to WPM, and "I never got a penny from them." And, unlike a lot of other people, he added, "I had some guests, quite a few, people who paid good money for my apartments."

"You had people; they paid the reservation services; you got no money; what happened to the money?" the writer asked. "Hell," Fred said, "you know how the Butcher people operated, always borrowing from Peter to pay Paul. When it came time to pay me, there was no Peter left."

A *News-Sentinel* story on July 30, 1985, indicated that WPM bankruptcy trustee John Harley Fowler had 4000 claims from renters and property owners. But prospects were not good. Fowler said that WPM's money had either "disappeared" or was owed to WPM by bankrupt people.

The tale of a world's fair gone wrong didn't stop with the small scale entrepreneurs. In spite of protestations to the contrary, Jake Butcher and C. H. Butcher, Jr., and their banks were known to be heavily involved in bankrolling fair-related projects. Bankruptcy documents, bank failures information, and post fair newspaper accounts indicated substantial losses in a number of instances for the Butchers, their associates, and their banks. A linen service collapsed into bankruptcy; parking lots were bare; restaurants fell short; two convenient store chains over-expanded and went bankrupt; housing units, campgrounds, trailer parks, and associated bus services were vastly over-built and collapsed, several going into bankruptcy. All three fair reservation service firms went bankrupt.

Some undetermined amount of the Butchers' money was in on the gold rush. And some of it went sour. But unfortunately, not much in the way of definitive statements can be made beyond that.

To be sure, opinion was there. Former UAB director Fred Langley, in a deposition for a court case (as carried in the *Knoxville Journal,* October 1, 1983), said that in his opinion the Butchers thought that if they could succeed in the World's Fair, it would bail them out. Ernie Beazley, by then with the *Wall Street Journal,* quoted a Knoxville banker in March 1983 as saying that he thought "Jake counted on the fair to bail him out." When that didn't work, he said, "there just weren't enough fingers to go in the dike."

From a different direction, the Federal Deposit Insurance Corporation (FDIC), shortly after UAB's failure, referred to bad World's Fair loans as one of the factors contributing to the fall. In a June 1987 interview, however, William Roelle, the FDIC's head liquidator in Knoxville, said that the World's Fair was of some consequence in the UAB collapse but not very much. Other problems had already overwhelmed the bank, he said.

Roelle's position is not incompatible with the opinion of Langley or of that banker cited by Beazley. Jake surely had reason to believe his banks were in trouble, and other evidence indicates that he clearly did know. Presumably also, he did think that "all the ships would rise" when the 1982 World's Fair tide rolled in.

Although evidence clearly indicates otherwise, Jake has always denied using the fair for his own benefit. His expressed statements indicate that the only connection between the fair and the bank failures was the amount of time he devoted to the fair at the expense of UAB. He became "totally obsessed" with the fair's success, he told the *Knoxville Journal's* Larry Daughtrey in an August 22, 1983, interview.

When Butcher later tried to use such inattention as a mitigating defense against criminal charges, the U.S. Attorney's office didn't buy it. Assistant U.S. Attorney Robert E. Simpson said in his pre-sentencing memorandum on the occasion of Jake's sentencing in June 1985 (as carried in the local press) that Jake Butcher "was in direct control and planned the fraudulent loans in which he was involved, and directed their cover-up." Jake may not have been steering the ship very well, but he was certainly on the bridge.

When all is said and done, the picture of the interrelationships between the banks and the fair is no doubt a highly complex one; but what we know at present can be said very simply. Definitive statements are not possible at this time, and perhaps never will be.

The Emptiness of Promises

Private projects such as those floated by the Butchers weren't the only enterprises that were taking a beating. As the fair process moved through time, a number of the major promises of the promotion saga started to unravel.

An early casualty, as noted in Book One, was the proposed $20 million Tennessee state pavilion. The city dramatically increased its fair-related debt with a $21 million project, part of which was to be converted into a convention center after the fair. The U.S. pavilion, at a public cost of $12.4 million, was not built in a manner which would allow easy conversion after the fair. The idea of an energy research center was quietly dropped and post-fair use became a question mark.

Time exposed the emptiness of other promises as well. After more than six years of fair boosterism the *Knoxville News-Sentinel* observed editorially in October 1983 that the World's Fair "did little or nothing to help this downtown business district." Annette Anderson, director of the Community Design Center, located in a neighborhood adjacent to the fair, told the Chicago-based *Neighborhood Works* that "the impact on neighborhoods was either zero or negative. . . . There's certainly no way to argue the fair benefited low-income inner-city people."

One also would be hard pressed to argue that the fair produced much in the way of permanent new jobs. Some ideas about promises and realities regarding jobs may be seen by looking again at that $9.9 million federal UDAG grant that was discussed in Book One. When the city's grant application was submitted, it had "documented" 37,000 new jobs, 17,000 of them permanent, that would flow from the grant. When the grant was awarded, an agreement was signed by HUD and the city calling for the creation of 2,115 new permanent jobs. Then in 1984 HUD's Office of Inspector General conducted an audit and found that 306 new jobs had resulted from grant projects.

(Surely the UDAG federal grant process in the Knoxville case deserves more treatment than it receives in this study. Knowledge gained earlier and reviewed here in Book One as well as information acquired in mid-1987 indicate that shenanigans of a high order occurred from the White House down through the city and the Expo Corporation to the recipients of the money. A recently received Audit Report (84-AT-242-1024), dated May 9, 1984, reveals, among other things, that: (1) the number of jobs created, as noted above, was dramatically lower than it was supposed to be; (2) developer construction cost certifications required by HUD, *if submitted*, involved "omissions, questionable claims and other . . . unexplained matters," with "certain cost claims" apparently being "extremely high"; (3) general contractor Franklin Haney received "Contractors overhead" of $3,253,819, when he "was apparently only a 'paper' general contractor"; (4) the grant implementation and oversight process was at best shoddy and inept. A case could easily be made for a lengthy manuscript on this grant. But the swim would be upstream in muddy water with many floating obstacles, something far beyond the reach of the present study.)

Perhaps even less impressive than the UDAG data are those for the broader Knoxville metropolitan area. In looking at either total employment or unemployment rates over the past ten years, one finds no evidence to indicate that Knoxville leaped over the performance of Tennessee's three other major Metropolitan Statistical Areas (MSA)--Memphis, Nashville, and Chattanooga. To the contrary, a case could be made that Knoxville has declined in the 1980's. Data from the Tennessee Department of Employment Security reveal that the other three MSA's, for example, have made more progress in reducing unemployment in the 1980's and two of the three had a higher percentage increase in total employment in the 1980's. But the variables are many and causal relations are slippery. Perhaps as good a guess as any would be the promoters' initial figure, before public relations inflation took over, of 5,000 new jobs, mostly of a temporary and moonlighting variety.

The fair's social impact on the broader Knoxville community is also difficult to assess. Without much question, public service agencies such as Traveler's Aid, Volunteers of America, the Salvation Army, and the Knox County Welfare Department were "flooded" with "individuals and families from coast to coast looking for jobs" that didn't exist, wrote Pamela Gentry of the

Knoxville Journal on July 30, 1982. As reported by Gentry: a 35-38 percent increase in case load, said one agency head; more than we've seen in my 13 years with the department, said another agency; some 600 persons a month, said still another agency. A lot of our clients, Nancy Reese of the Mental Health and Crisis Center for Visitors told Gentry, thought "the fair was a pot of gold at the end of the rainbow." The Center's policy is to try "to find day labor for them so they can earn their way home," she said.

Clearly, it wasn't just people looking for jobs who ran into difficulty. There were also the victims of crime. As compared with the same period in 1981, the Knoxville police reported, the arrest rate from May through October 1982 saw substantial increases in a number of categories. Some rates, it is true, were down: murder was down by 22 percent; robbery, by 20 percent; burglary, by 21 percent. But generally, arrests were up substantially: larceny was up by 368 percent; motor vehicle theft, by 177 percent; driving under the influence, by 99 percent; rape, by 80 percent; and aggravated assault, by 202 percent.

But for all the human tragedy that was no doubt reflected in increased demands on social service agencies and in increased criminal activity, the fair's overall social impact on the broader Knoxville community seemed to be somewhat similar to the economic impact. Nothing much materialized off-site. Things were different, some, but the fair was "down there," and for those who weren't, well, they sort of did the same old things.

As opening day neared, KIEE officials, in anticipation of massive clogging of the interstates as well as local streets, first asked local people to hold back, to come later; but then, in the face of hostile reactions, reversed themselves. But neither their panic action nor their retraction seemed to make much difference. On the morning of opening day, Jim Dykes wrote, "there was hardly any traffic downtown." It would be a mistake to say it stayed that way every day, all day, for the fair's duration. But that would be more accurate than what the 1982 World's Fair officials expected or what I expected or what many off-site entrepreneurs expected.

The miscalculations apparently came from the ratio of buses to cars as a means of transportation to the fair. Robert Womack of the *Journal* wrote on July 30, 1982, that Expo's transportation consultant, Barton-Aschman Associates of Evanston, Illinois, predicted that two-thirds of the people would come by car. Actually, Womack said, citing downtown parking lot officials, the ratio may have been the reverse with some two-thirds coming by tour and other buses. Whether this is an accurate assessment or not, the consequences of the limited amount of off-site activities were formidable. For the broader social order, they were generally positive; for the off-site economic enterprises they were frequently disastrous.

No "Manna from Heaven"

Another group that got caught up in the off-site impact vacuum was a number of city employees. Their plight grew from the realization by city officials some two weeks after the fair closed that tax revenues from amusement rides and off-site entertainment events were going to be substantially lower than budgeted. A freeze on hiring and purchase of new equipment for the remaining seven months of the fiscal year was implemented in mid-November. And then, as Christmas approached, over 150 city workers were cut from the payroll as the city began dealing with almost $2 million of red ink.

Of substantially more importance for the city as a whole as we moved on into the post-fair period was some $44 million in fair-related debt, all in short-term notes designed to defer permanent solutions until well after the fair was over.

Back before the fair, then Mayor Randy Tyree told the West Palm Beach *Post* that "we will have absolutely no trouble . . . repaying these notes." A year after the fair ended, Mayor Kyle Testerman, the *News-Sentinel* reported, was trying to avoid what he said would otherwise be "a massive tax increase."

In dealing with the new debt, said then city finance director Rick Dulaney in a February 1985 interview, the city cut services, used some one-time revenue sources, left $9.5 million in fair-related debts to be dealt with later, and (by far the most important) refinanced $50.2 million in old debt.

It is difficult to overestimate the significance of the debt refinancing scheme. Analysis of the city's official statement for the 1984 refinancing bond sale reveals that the *additional* cost of the old debt over the 20 year life of the new bonds is $60.4 million. To illustrate further, under the old debt retirement structure the city in the year 2001 would have been making a total principal and interest payment of $518,000. Under the new structure the payment will be $10.5 million.

On the other hand, by stretching out the old debt the city was able to issue other bonds to cover 1982 World's Fair related debts and yet keep current debt service payments at a tolerable level. Without the refinancing, the city wrote in its official statement, dated April 18, 1984, the city's debt service requirements "would exceed the maximum annual debt service which is considered fiscally responsible by city officials."

But the cost of the refinancing scheme was high in terms of both dollars paid out and the city's future financial flexibility. The city is now locked into a debt repayment schedule until the year 2005 that essentially prohibits any substantial increase in future borrowing for public improvements.

In any case, as a result of such manipulations the city avoided a tax increase in 1984. But "we only deferred it," said Mayor Testerman. The problem, he told the *News-Sentinel* in October 1984, won't be cured by "some manna from heaven." Taxes increased by 14 percent in 1985. Thereafter the tax rate stabilized, partly because of reductions in the number of employees but mainly, said city finance director Randy Vineyard in a June 1987 interview, because of savings that came from privatizing garbage collection and, especially, from turning over the city school system to the county government, thereby avoiding the consequences of dealing with the elimination of federal revenue-sharing funds and other one-time funds in the city's last education budget.

Even with all the problems involved, dealing with finances may be easier than curing the city's bad reputation with some undetermined number of visitors. The fair, promoters were prone to say, would put Knoxville on the map. To some extent it surely did so. And generally, one would suspect, the visitors' image of Knoxville and its people was more positive than negative. But without question the centralized reservation system was a dismal failure for the fair organization and for thousands of visitors.

About a month after the fair closed, the state of Tennessee filed a consumer fraud suit against KIEE and its reservation agencies. In an out-of-court settlement of March 1983, the accused, the *Journal* reported, admitted the system failed to make refunds, double-charged customers, and provided inadequate accommodations, with some tourists being booked "into rooms of such poor quality as to be uninhabitable."

The settlement provided for the establishment of a claims fund of $900,000 to be administered to some 3,000 complainants by the state's Consumer Affairs Division and the Attorney General's office. Eighty thousand dollars was put in the fund with the remainder to be entered pending the outcome of two court suits. Some two and a half years later settlements were reached in the court cases. Another year passed and partial payments started going out to those who could verify their claims.

In a June 1987 interview, Steve Hart of the state Attorney General's office said that things were finally winding down. The fund grew to $412,000, and checks started going out to 3,010 claimants in September 1986, almost four years after the fair ended. Claims up to $900 were paid at 42 cents on the dollar in one suit and at 48 cents on the dollar in others, Hart stated. He also observed that many claims against the reservation services were disallowed because of inadequate supporting evidence. In addition, he said, nothing was done about some 2000-3000 filed monetary complaints against individual motels outside the central reservation system. "We just didn't have the manpower or the money to deal with them," he said. Nor were they able to do anything about thousands of other complaints that did not involve monetary claims.

"It was just awful," Melinda Fields of the Consumer Affairs Division, said in an early 1985 interview. Apparently, things didn't get a lot better as the years passed. "Some of the people," Steve Hart said, "became very frustrated." Their hostility "spilled over beyond the fair and housing to the state and everybody in it." They just don't "understand our authority," said Hart. "And there is simply not enough money there."

For many, to be sure, the fair wasn't very fair.

CHAPTER 7
The Shovel Brigade

"On Top of the World"

When the 1982 World's Fair came to a close on October 31, 1982, some of the problems noted in the last chapter were not known. A lot were. But the mode of operation of the promoters didn't allow them to recognize shortcomings, to recognize problems.

At the fair's closing ceremonies, the *Knoxville Journal* reported, Mayor Randy Tyree was beaming. "We're a unique success story that will go down in history," he said. And, said Charles H. Dean, Jr., Tennessee Valley Authority (TVA) board chairman, the best is yet to come. Post-fair development is "going to make downtown Knoxville."

And then came Jake Butcher, the fair's chairman and most prominent promoter. Jake, UPI reported, was jubilant. "We did it," he told the cheering crowd. "You ain't a-braggin' when you gone and done it."

Jake surely appeared to have it all. The helicopter-hopping banker was worth a self-proclaimed $40 million. He had been a guest in the White House of President Jimmy Carter. Carter had been a guest at Whirlwind, Butcher's east Tennessee mansion ("a cross between Tara and Southfork" said Victoria McDonald in *Knoxville Magazine*). Jake knew the high and the mighty of Tennessee and the surrounding states. He had political power and he used it--in Washington, in Nashville, in Knoxville.

To be sure, failures had slipped in. Butcher had run for governor twice and lost, in the Democratic primary in 1974 and then in the general election of 1978. But generally the story was success.

Indeed, *Success* magazine in January 1982 carried a Butcher-World's Fair story entitled "On Top of the World." The reason for Butcher's success is clear, said author Jerry DeLaughter. Butcher has "savvy."

"I see very few people with much savvy," said Butcher. "Savvy has a lot to do with instincts, personality, judgment. I guess you can develop savvy, but it helps to be born with it," Butcher continued.

The author was impressed. "His banks," said DeLaughter, "are burgeoning successes, his personal fortune is secure."

Butcher's media image spread even further. "To the Top" was the label on a *People Weekly* story about this "self-made millionaire and visionary entrepreneur" who had used "backslapping flair," "whirlwind energy," and "brash self-confidence," not only to secure himself a "place among the rich and powerful of Tennessee," but also to "ramrod" the 1982 World's Fair "from conception to completion."

"Leveraged" to the Hilt

But even while the band played "Rocky Top" and guests sipped champagne, a small army of banking examiners from the Federal Deposit Insurance Company (FDIC), a federal agency responsible for regulating member banks and insuring their individual deposits, was descending upon UAB Knoxville, C&C Bank of Knox County, and other banks in the banking empires of Jake and C. H. Butcher, Jr.

Since the beginning of their banking rise, the Butcher banks, theoretically divided into two separate systems since 1980, had been examined periodically by appropriate federal and state agencies. But examinations before November 1, 1982, had occurred one bank at a time, with sufficient advance knowledge available to enable the Butcher brothers to anticipate the arrival of the examiners. This time it was a secret attack with some 180 examiners descending on the two Butcher systems at once. Just a "routine" exam, a UAB spokesman told the *Journal* at the end of January 1983.

But the examination was anything but routine, either for the FDIC or for Jake and C. H. Butcher, Jr., and many of their associates. When all the banks were hit at once, said the FDIC's James L. Sexton to the *Journal's* Joe Krakoviak in late February, we got "an idea of the total credit obligations of the creditors."

The FDIC had been suspicious earlier. Now it knew it was dealing with a disaster. On February 14, 1983, UAB Knoxville, on order of the FDIC, was declared insolvent, closed by the state banking commissioner because of "large and unusual loan losses" and "unsound banking practices," and sold off to First Tennessee Bank. The bank had vast sums of loan money concentrated in the hands of so-called "insiders," people directly associated with the bank, and others closely associated otherwise with Jake Butcher. Large quantities of loans were backed by little or in many instances no collateral. Several different loans would be backed by the same collateral. Loans were being extended to people who already had high levels of outstanding loans. Many of the major loans were backed by bank stock that became worthless when a bank collapsed. The canoe was overloaded with people who were riding too high.

One year to the day before UAB's collapse the president of another Knoxville bank was telling the *Atlanta Constitution* about Butcher and UAB: "Some of these high rollers . . . are going to come back to earth." "A brakeless banker," I had called Jake a few weeks earlier. Sometimes a high roller needs brakes. But this wasn't Jake's explanation.

"The bank wasn't insolvent. The bank was never insolvent," Butcher told the Memphis *Commercial Appeal* two days after the bank collapsed. "The (FDIC) bureaucracy," he said, "just got a steamroller going and rolled over me." The investigation, Butcher told the *Journal,* was politically motivated. And his man at City Hall, Mayor Randy Tyree, agreed. It was "a rush to judgment," said Tyree to the *Commercial Appeal.* More time would have been available "if Jimmy Carter had been in the White House or there was a Democratic governor." Perhaps so, but the facts that emerged later seem indisputable.

"It was numbers, not politics," said former UAB director Lindsay Young.

And for all the complexity of the Butcher system, the overriding fact about the "numbers" was a simple one. Everything, everyone, was interlocked and "leveraged" to the hilt.

In the wake of the fall of UAB, ten more Butcher-related banks, including C. H. Butcher, Jr.'s, premier institution, C&C Bank of Knox County, were declared insolvent, closed, sold off, and reopened under new ownership. It was the same interlocking story, ten times over.

Collectively, the closing of the Butcher banks was the largest bank failure since the Great Depression. But it was even bigger. As some were being declared insolvent, others were simply being sold off. The Butchers' 27-bank system was gone. In addition, C. H. Butcher, Jr.'s, Southern Industrial Banking Corporation (SIBC), a state loan company and technically not a bank, was declared bankrupt. Unlike the other institutions in the Butcher collapse, where each depositor's savings were insured up to $100,000, SIBC had no insurance on its $52 million in deposits.

Given the interlocking nature of everything, the fall of the banks could not occur in isolation. Within months Jake and C. H. Butcher, Jr., their wives, and a number of associates were declared bankrupt.

"If I've done anything wrong," said Butcher to *News-Sentinel* reporter Carson Brewer in August 1983, "I didn't intend to. And whatever I've done wrong, I want to make it right if it takes me the rest of my life."

"My commitment," Butcher said, "is to pay everybody I owe."

Even as he spoke Butcher was settling into his newly acquired $675,000 home in Florida, while his attorneys were opposing the efforts of creditors who were asking the bankruptcy judge to appoint a trustee to protect their interests. They knew of what they spoke.

The Fog Was Thick

As the complex Butcher system disintegrated and former associates moved to cover their civil and criminal tracks, federal investigations, court actions and media coverage hit record highs. Everyone seemed to be trying to get back money or keep from paying out money. The Butchers and their former banks and business enterprises were center stage.

Securities and Exchange Commission agents were at work. Internal Revenue Service agents were at work. FDIC investigators were at work. Creditors and court appointed bankruptcy estate trustees (responsible for accumulating the available assets and distributing them to the creditors) were at work. And the Federal Bureau of Investigation was at work.

Everyone was looking and asking. Answers weren't easy to come by. Leon Ridenour called 1983 the "Year of the Fifth," as the number of refusals to answer or to provide records on grounds of the Fifth Amendment protection against self-incrimination went through the ceiling.

But as time went on, the nature of the Butcher operations started to emerge. Surely not all the way, however, as there were too many people, too many angles, too much action, too many Dempster Dumpsters. If the definitive work is ever written, it won't be definitive. Perhaps no one knows this better than the personnel at the Federal Deposit Insurance Corporation.

The FDIC had experienced problems with UAB Knoxville going all the way back to 1976 when the bank was first acquired by Jake Butcher. But FDIC words of wisdom and caution then and later didn't seem to have much impact. The number of banks grew, each in succession acquired through the borrowing power of its predecessors. Trouble ahead? "Out-dollar it," C. H. used to say, stated his right hand manipulator, David Crabtree. Squeeze more money out. Find another bank. Ever more dubious banking practices, the FDIC later discovered, became increasingly prominent. But questionable loans and insider operations were crucial to FDIC bank examiners only if they were seen in their full scope.

In order to keep bank examiners from knowing the extent of bad loans the Butcher banks engaged in loan shifting whereby a bank under scrutiny would "sell" questionable loans to other banks for what at least appeared to be solid assets, with the understanding that the exchange would be reversed after the bank examiners left.

Armed with documents from a Kentucky court case concerning Butcher bank practices before the fall, Georgianna Vines of the *News-Sentinel* (September 3, 1984) quoted a letter from Stephen Hagood, the president of C. H. Butcher, Jr.'s, C&C Bank of Knox County, to Charles R. Watson, Jr., chief executive officer of UAB Knoxville. C&C would purchase $20 million in loans from UAB, Hagood wrote, with an agreement that the loans would be repurchased within 60 days "or when the bank examiners have completed their examination, whichever is sooner."

But the fog was thick around the exchange. After following a rather circuitous path, Vines discovered that C&C "bought $20 million in participation [loans] from UAB Knoxville with money borrowed from UAB Knoxville."

Another case emerged in the *Journal's* November 1983 coverage of a U.S. House of Representatives' sub-committee report. In order to escape the scrutiny of bank regulators UAB Knoxville "sold" $16 million in bad loans to Southern Industrial Banking Corporation (SIBC), with SIBC paying for the loans with a $16 million check drawn on its account in C&C Hawkins County. After the fall, regulators "learned Southern Industrial had only $10 in the Hawkins County account."

"You can do interesting things with a chain of banks," observed William H. Roelle, the FDIC liquidation manager in Knoxville, in a June 1987 interview.

And the Butchers surely engaged in many interesting things. But were these technologies discovered by the Butchers or were they already known to FDIC regulators? Just what did the regulators know about the Butcher banking operations--and when did they know it? And most important of all, why did the FDIC wait so long before launching a full-scale, system-wide examination of the Butcher brothers' banks?

A complete picture of the FDIC's relationships with UAB is certainly not available to this writer. But certain information is. In particular, a "confidential" internal FDIC "staff briefing" memorandum, dated March 11, 1983, raises some interesting issues, as it summarizes the FDIC's examination history of UAB going all the way back to UAB's conversion to a state charter bank (from a federal charter bank) on November 1, 1976.

FDIC records reveal that the FDIC examiner at the first UAB examination in April 1977 was concerned enough to note that Jake Butcher "dominated policy formulation." The examiner was also worried about "excessive" compensation for Butcher, and about "heavy Director, Officer, and Employee indebtedness." An examination a year later raised concerns about "heavy loan losses, weak earnings, and high volume of insider loans." All of these things remained as concerns of a January 1979 examination, with an additional item of "massive" asset deterioration thrown in. A June 1980 examination "revealed some improvement in the bank's condition," but problems were still there. And then in November 1981 an examination "revealed a reversal of virtually all the improvements noted at the 1980 examination." This examination, the FDIC's March 1983 memorandum stated, "suggested [that] problem status was approaching." And the regulatory body started to shift into high gear, with discussions and directions and warnings, and ultimately with the full-system examination that began on November 1, 1982.

Perhaps it is significant that the November 1981 examination was the first under the Reagan administration. An assessment of the situation is not easy, but the available information suggests that it wasn't politics that brought the Butchers down but rather politics that kept them up--until that final 11-bank cataclysmic collapse that started at UAB on February 14, 1983. In any case, the FDIC surely had reason to be more than a little suspicious of Jake Butcher and aware of the possibility that loan shifting and other means were being used to conceal the real status of bank assets and liabilities in the combined operation of Jake's 5-bank system and C. H.'s 22-bank system. If you know "you can do interesting things with a chain of banks," wouldn't you suspect that Jake and Jesse and C. H. would be doing them?

The above is not meant to suggest that Jake got on the phone and said, "Hey, President Jimmy, those FDIC boys are on my back," with Jimmy in turn calling FDIC director William Isaac and saying, "Bill, get off Jake's back." Peddling influence down the administrative ladder--everywhere from here to Timbuktu--can be a very subtle thing. FDIC personnel knew who President Carter was, and who Senator Jim Sasser was, and who Jake Butcher was. Remember the message of that FBI agent: we have to watch out for the "sensitive" political cases. You just know where it's at, brother. And frequently administrators act accordingly.

"Their Own Bank Within a Bank"

The problem with the Butchers, however, did not involve just their banks and moving money back and forth between them. There was, after all, a reason for the "bad" loans. Numerous bits and pieces appeared in the local press in both 1983 and 1984. Then in January 1985 Jake Butcher's bankruptcy trustee and the FDIC attorney were before Bankruptcy Judge Clive Bare arguing that Butcher had committed fraud in the accumulation of his debts and therefore should not be forgiven them.

As reported in the Knoxville newspapers on January 17 and 18, the story went as follows. By using the names of various firms and fronts, FDIC attorney John Neal said, Butcher had taken out loans from his bank and then through various routes had eventually gotten the money back into his own hands. In one case, a $2.7 million note was issued to Franklin Haney Construction Company of Chattanooga with the name of company officer Jeff Leonard being forged on the loan document. The money went not to Haney's company but to Butcher's JFB Petroleum and Land Company.

Bankruptcy trustee John H. Bailey III added that some $18 million had flowed through JFB in 1982. He had been able to trace most of the money into personal uses by Butcher, Bailey said. But not all. Bailey stated that $2.1 million "just disappeared" from the record. "We don't know where it went," he said.

C. H. Butcher, Jr., was also in the game. It went like this, said the U.S. Attorney in a sentencing memorandum of May 1987. C. H. would direct the approval of a loan to some other individual or entity and then move the funds into his own control. No disclosure of the ultimate user would be made, and since C. H. was doing the directing, no credit or collateral investigations would occur and the loan would receive automatic approval by the particular board involved. The U.S. Attorney summarized one such case:

> On September 24, 1982, Butcher, Jr. directed employees of Knox Federal to process a loan for Shirley Butcher in the amount of $1,707,527 allegedly for real estate development. Instead, Butcher diverted $1,400,000 of the proceeds for use as the earnest money deposit in the purchase of a Florida savings and loan. Ultimately, when the purchase fell through, Butcher transferred the funds to the United Southern, Ltd., account in the Grand Cayman Islands. The loan was never paid back, and presently the funds remain unaccounted for.

"The Butchers," said SIBC bankruptcy trustee Tom DuVoisin in a June 1987 interview, "were operating their own bank within a bank." It was like "two different animals, two modes of operation."

And there was a theory at work, or so thought one former UAB director. Fred Langley's conception, as stated in a court deposition, was as follows (*Journal,* October 1, 1983): "The theory was, from Jake Butcher, 'you can't go broke in a bank. The only way you could go broke in a bank is to shovel the money out the door.' "

A House of Cards

As the FDIC went about the business of trying to collect the loans of fallen banks, and bankruptcy trustees went about the business of trying to accumulate the assets of fallen stars, certain images emerged. The Butcher group may have been movers, but a lot of what they were moving was fiction. As the Butchers fell, presumed money just evaporated into thin air.

Originally the FDIC, as it closed UAB Knoxville, estimated its loan losses would be $60 million. But as the interlocking nature of the banks and the multitude of bankruptcies became clear, the loan loss estimate for UAB was sharply increased, ultimately reaching a mid-1987 estimate of over $300 million. C.H.'s C&C of Knox County was estimated to have losses of just under $90 million. Collectively, the closed Butcher brother banks had estimated losses of over $623 million. (All data from the pre-sentencing memorandum for C. H. Butcher, Jr., by Assistant U.S. Attorney Guy W. Blackwell, filed on May 20, 1987, at U.S. District Court, Knoxville.)

On the personal side, also, money vaporized. Before their fall Jake and C. H. Butcher, Jr., each claimed that he had a net worth of some $40 million. As the number of bankruptcies mounted, the substance, the reality, of wealth was revealed. The Butcher brothers were declared bankrupt in mid-1983. A few months later, bankruptcy documents reveal, Jake had unsecured claims of over $208 million against his bankruptcy estate. As of June 30, 1987, his bankruptcy estate trustee had been able to collect assets of only $5.6 million.

C. H. Butcher, Jr., has $234 million in unsecured claims, said bankruptcy trustee James R. Martin in a July 1987 interview. At that time Martin had accumulated assets of $7.7 million to meet those claims. But this case is like an octopus, he said. "It never stops wiggling." When it does stop, perhaps by the end of 1988, Martin said, he expects to have the legitimate claims down to $100-120 million and to have collected assets of some $10 million that can be used to meet those claims. "We should be able to pay about nine or ten cents on the dollar," Martin said.

A "paper fortune," wrote *Journal* reporter Robert Womack. Everybody owed everybody and nobody had real money.

"People ask me," Jake Butcher reportedly stated, "how I made so much money so fast, and I tell them it's because I owe so much money. You get used to it," he explained. "It's like when you start going barefooted in the spring: for the first few days, those gravel really hurt, but then your feet toughen up and you don't notice it." (As quoted in David M. Dickson and Chris Lamb, *ICON*, October 1983).

But others did notice it. And in due time the pieces started to come together.

A Dealer

The picture painted thus far surely suggests that someone, somewhere down the line, would feel the long arm of the law. The first to do so was master arranger David A. Crabtree, an accountant turned financier with long-term associations with the Butchers.

"Crabtree was the architect for front companies for both Butcher brothers' business interests, a means of hiding insider loans from regulators," wrote Thomas F.

Chester and Alan Hall in the *Journal* on October 28, 1983. With loans of at least $120 million from the Butchers' banking network, reported Chester and Hall, Crabtree ran some 60 Butcher-related companies from Suite 2136 at UAB Plaza. [The article by Chester and Hall was one of a long series in late October and early November 1983 on the fall of the Butcher banks by seven reporters from the *Knoxville Journal* and the *Nashville Tennessean,* two Gannett chain newspapers. Now available as a collected set, "Borrowed Money, Borrowed Time" remains the foremost single piece of work on the bank failures.]

With the collapse of UAB, Crabtree was forced into bankruptcy in August 1983. Ultimately, claims against his bankruptcy estate reached a total of $107 million. But bankruptcy trustee D. Broward Craig had only been able to accumulate assets of $6.3 million, according to his most recent report of April 1987.

Singularly uncooperative with his bankruptcy trustee from the beginning, Crabtree on one occasion spent eight days in the county jail, on order of the bankruptcy court. He failed to produce records. He failed to answer more than a thousand questions about his finances, pleading his Fifth Amendment right against self-incrimination.

Even while in the throes of all this, Crabtree continued to be the consummate mover of money. In March 1984 he was indicted by a federal grand jury on four counts of allegedly hiding $945,000 in a bank account in the Cayman Islands.

The federal prosecutors and Crabtree apparently decided they needed one another. A plea-bargain agreement was reached in May 1984, over the objections of Crabtree's creditors and his bankruptcy trustee. Crabtree was given protection against any further prosecution for past financial dealings. In return, he agreed to cooperate with other prosecutions and to plead guilty to four counts of bankruptcy fraud, for which he received a 15-year sentence. This is "one of the largest (sentences) received in recent years in a white collar crime," said U.S. Attorney John Gill *(Journal,* May 11, 1984).

At a meeting with his creditors shortly after the plea agreement Crabtree was asked a familiar question. Where are the records? Now obligated to cooperate, Crabtree observed that after UAB had fallen, his funds had been cut off and he didn't need most of the records anymore. So six days later, Crabtree said, "I just threw them away . . . in a Dempster Dumpster" *(News-Sentinel,* May 23, 1984).

Crabtree had participated in many deals in his 14-year association with the Butchers, wrote the *Journal's* Joe Krakoviak on May 11, 1984, but his plea agreement "may have been his slickest deal yet." In exchange for a 15-year sentence "he will not be prosecuted for his part in the failure of 10 Butcher banks and the disappearance of millions of dollars in loans."

Moreover, the assumption in mid-1984 was that Crabtree, under existing parole policy, would serve no more than two to two-and-a-half years. "David is very anxious to put this matter behind him and start rebuilding his life," said Crabtree attorney Robert Richie *(News-Sentinel,* January 2, 1985).

Jake Folded

As David was starting "to put this matter behind him," decision time was rapidly approaching for Jake and two of his colleagues. On November 13, 1984, a federal grand jury in Knoxville indicted Jake Butcher and his long-time confidant and "alter ego" Jesse Barr on 23 counts of bank fraud, 20 counts of making false entries in bank records, and one count of conspiracy to commit bank fraud, all at UAB Knoxville. Jack Patrick, a relatively unknown vice president at UAB, joined Butcher and Barr in 31 of the charges.

"The indictments," as described by *Tennessean* reporters Larry Daughtrey and James Pratt, "spell out a tale of repeated swindling and high level spending that helped bring about the doom of a dozen Tennessee banks. When Butcher accounts ran dry they were replenished with Butcher bank loans made to non-existent companies or to companies whose officers' signatures were forged. In all, the Knoxville indictments charged, $14.9 million was siphoned to the personal use of Butcher and Barr." Bank records were falsified in order to conceal the real beneficiaries from bank regulators.

"I am innocent," Butcher said in a prepared statement carried in the local press. "And with the help of God and the faith of friends, we will continue to fight with courage and dignity."

Indictments followed indictments, as prosecutors cut a trail to other Butcher banks. By March 7, 1985, Jake, the *Journal* reported, had been indicted five times in three different cities and was faced with 92 counts of bank fraud involving $20 million that had been illegally directed from his banks into his control, and nine counts of income tax evasion, involving non-payment of taxes on 25 "loans" totaling $40.8 million channelled to him by associates Jesse Barr and G. W. Ridenour, Jr., through sham companies, and through forged signatures on notes hypothetically arranged by real companies.

Jake was in trouble.

Three days before his first trial was to begin on April 22, 1985, Jake and the U.S. Attorney's office, as reported in the local press, reached a plea agreement covering the entirety of the charges. Jake would plead guilty to a total of 20 counts of bank fraud and tax evasion. In return, he would receive a term of no more than 20 years in prison.

In his pre-sentencing memorandum to the court in Knoxville, Butcher's attorney, James F. Sanders of Nashville, searched for a way to get Jake off light, hopefully with a three-year term. According to press reports in early June, Sanders argued that Jake had already suffered for his crimes: from his detection, his bankruptcy, his indictments, his loss of honor and respect. And he surely would serve time in jail. But, said Sanders, "it is the fact of incarceration, not the length," that will deter others from doing what Jake did.

Jake Butcher, his attorney argued, "is as far removed from the criminal mentality as one can imagine." Jake "is a kind and simple soul." He was facing the pressure of debts and of World's Fair leadership. The crimes Jake committed, Sanders said, resulted from "interludes of insanity."

"Yeah, he's crazy. Crazy over money," said Phil Williams of WIMZ, a local rock station.

The pre-sentencing memorandum of Assistant U.S. Attorney Robert E. Simpson was closer to Phil's opinion. Butcher, Simpson said, used fraudulently obtained loans to pay his own debts, to further his own career and image, to cover his political campaign expenses, and to "maintain his lavish and luxurious lifestyle." And Jake knew what he was doing. He was "in direct control, planned the fraudulent loans . . . and directed their coverup and concealment."

Jake Butcher, Simpson said, is "a sophisticated criminal in a pin-striped suit who undertook to steal millions and millions of dollars from the depositors of the banks which he controlled." And he should pay the price to demonstrate something to others in positions of trust and to restore the faith of the people in the society. Jake, Simpson said, should receive a sentence "far above" the "normal" for such crimes. Jake should receive the maximum of 20 years, as provided in the plea agreement.

On June 3, 1985, Senior U.S. District Court Judge William K. Thomas handed down the first of Butcher's four sentences. Speaking for 45 minutes, the local press reported, Judge Thomas told Jake that a "deterrent force," a "clarion message," had to be delivered. And "public confidence" had to be restored. Nothing less would do. He gave Jake a 20-year sentence under a sentencing/parole rule whereby Jake would have to serve at least one-third of his sentence--six years and eight months.

Butcher reported to the medium-security Federal Prison Camp at Atlanta, Georgia, on September 3, 1985.

A month later Jake sent a six-page handwritten letter to Judge Thomas asking for a reduction in sentence. (Released to the press and carried in full in the *Journal* January 9, 1986.)

"Your honor," Jake said, "I will make no more excuses for my crime." And then he wrote:

> I am so ashamed. All these people had such faith in me and I thought I could provide to the people of Tennessee the most progressive banking system in the country. I wanted to have Knoxville recognized nationally through the World's Fair. I wanted to be governor of Tennessee and do so much for all those people. . . . I should have stopped. The means [do] not justify the ends. . . . If only I would have told everyone, it can't be done, I can't do everything, [I'm] not superman.

"Your honor," Jake concluded, "I want to repent. I hope you will give me this opportunity to live again."

The response of U.S. Attorney John Gill to Butcher's plea, as reported in the *Journal* of January 1, 1986, was sharp. Butcher, Gill said, is "the biggest thief in the history of the state of Tennessee."

And Jesse Barr and G.W. Ridenour, Jr.

Jake could not go down alone. "Alter-ego" Jesse Barr was the mastermind, said federal prosecutors. He was with Jake on the bulk of the bank fraud and income tax conspiracy charges, 94 in all. But for Jesse, it was old hat. He was making his second trip to the bar of justice. For action undertaken while he was executive vice-president of

Union Planters Bank in Memphis, as reported by Ernie Beazley of the *Journal* in August 1980, Barr "was convicted September 30, 1976, on 25 of 31 federal counts of bank fraud ranging from embezzlement to misapplication and conversion of nearly $17 million . . . to his own personal use."

In sentencing Barr, Beazley continued, U.S. District Court Judge Bailey Brown noted that Barr's conviction and sentence would discourage others from "dipping into the till." People, the Judge said, "sometimes feel and rightly, I think, that the little people . . . get in trouble and have the book thrown at them while the big boys can get a lot of money and there's nothing done to them."

The judge, of course, had a point back in 1976. Indeed, a congressional report, as covered by the *News-Sentinel* on September 22, states that both the bank regulators and the Justice Department have "an 'uneven' record in prosecuting bank insiders," even though the FBI estimates that during 1982 eight times more money "was stolen by insiders and other employees of financial institutions than was stolen through bank robberies and burglaries."

There is, I suspect, a lesson here someplace. Jesse Barr did go off to prison. After serving one year of a five-year sentence in a "middle-class" federal prison at Elgin Air Force Base ("summer camp," Barr said to the *News-Sentinel's* James Cole), Barr was released on parole.

Although prohibited from working for an insured bank as a result of his bank fraud convictions, Barr was surely there at UAB and quite prominent. Too many people knew too much. Jesse, like Jake, took the plea bargain route. Jesse argued that he hadn't received the money. It had gone to Jake. But he got 18 years under the one-third-time sentencing rule and while serving his minimum of six years at a medium security facility in Lexington, Kentucky, was teaching investment strategy to his colleagues.

The ending was dramatically different in the case of prominent millionaire lawyer and close Butcher associate G. W. Ridenour, Jr. Ridenour, by this time bankrupt, was accused in March 1985 of assisting Jake in his income tax evasion conspiracy as well as filing false returns himself. But Ridenour did not choose the plea bargain route. He was tried, found guilty, and sentenced to 20 years. His close ties to Butcher operations led many to assume that he would ultimately be charged with bank fraud. It was not to be. On February 1, 1986, Ridenour drove to a point on

I-75 near the top of Jellico Mountain and killed himself, with a 12-gauge shotgun blast to the head, four hours before he was to report to a federal prison at Montgomery, Alabama.

And C. H. and Others

On the heels of the Ridenour tragedy, C. H. Butcher, Jr., was arrested and jailed in Knoxville on February 6, charged in a 26-count federal indictment with mail, wire, and securities fraud regarding the operations and collapse of Southern Industrial Banking Corporation. The U.S. Attorney's office asked, and the U.S. Magistrate concurred, that Butcher be held without bond because of the risk that he might flee the country.

C. H., as it turned out, was tried and acquitted of all counts in the SIBC indictment. Although without funds, C. H. had not been without friends, and through their financial efforts had been able to hire famed Georgia "country lawyer" Bobby Lee Cook. Bobby Lee apparently had been able to point a finger at David Crabtree, our old friend and C. H. associate, and convince the jurors that David was the villain.

But C. H.'s victory was a hollow one. The indictments kept coming--69 counts of bankruptcy fraud and conspiracy, three counts of money laundering, and 21 counts charging bank fraud. And he brought others with him on a number of the charges--his wife, Shirley; his son, C.H. III (Butch); his father, C.H., Sr.; Butch's girlfriend, Terri Atchley; associate Gary Long; Union County Bank clerk Emma Bailey; and David Crabtree.

This time around C. H. Butcher, Jr., didn't have Bobby Lee Cook, but he did have prominent Atlanta lawyer Ed Garland. It was all for naught. As the trial date neared and the facts stared Ed in the face, C. H. got religion. "In coming to terms with these moral issues," he said in a presentencing letter to U.S. District Judge Thomas A. Higgins, "I went back to my Christian Childhood and remembered the lessons my mother taught me" (*Journal*, June 1, 1987). On April 7, 1987, C. H. Butcher, Jr., as recounted in the U.S. Attorney's pre-sentencing memorandum of May 20, entered guilty pleas to five counts of bankruptcy fraud and conspiracy, two counts of money-laundering, and five counts of bank fraud.

In addition, Butcher pleaded guilty to charges in three other indictments: (1) bank fraud and tax fraud conspiracy in an indictment charging Congressman Harold

Ford of Memphis and Jake and C. H. Butcher, Jr., and others, with an influence-peddling scheme; (2) tax fraud conspiracy in a scheme whereby "Butcher agreed to pay off over $300,000 of [Joe] Duncan's [the son of East Tennessee Congressman John Duncan] debt in exchange for Butcher receiving control of Knox Federal"; and (3) tax fraud and tax fraud conspiracy in that very same SIBC case in which Bobby Lee Cook had labored so hard for an acquittal. In a case involving bizarre people doing bizarre things in bizarre ways, this last was truly bizarre. C. H. had pleaded guilty to charges for which he had already been tried and found not guilty in a jury trial.

In exchange for all this pleading, the U.S. Attorney office agreed to ask for no more than 25 years for C. H. Butcher, Jr. And he asked for it all: C. H. was the "consummate white-collar criminal." He was even worse than Jake, the U.S. Attorney said.

Before the federal judges had a chance to sentence C.H., he had also pleaded guilty to 13 counts of a 16 count state indictment associated with his operation of SIBC. The lecturing started--by a state judge, by two federal judges. When the dust settled, C.H. Butcher, Jr., had been sentenced to five years on the state charges and 20 years on the federal charges, with no minimum or maximum guaranteed. At this writing in mid-1987, C.H. is in the state's Silverdale Workhouse in Hamilton County, where he will spend several months before moving into the care of the federal prison system for an expected seven or eight years.

For C.H. the plea agreement perhaps was a bargain. The nine failed banks directly under his control were expected by the FDIC to have total loan losses of $292,573,875, with a total of 185 criminal referrals being made to federal investigative agencies regarding the banks' operations. He also had a hand in Jake's two failed banks with loan losses expected to exceed $330 million. His bankrupt SIBC has caused years of incredible agony for many of its approximately 7000 investors, with some 2500 of them still dangling and collectively expecting millions of dollars in losses. C.H. and his wife had fought James R. Martin, the trustee of their bankruptcy estates, all the way in his attempt to recover hidden assets that could be used to pay off part of more than $200 million in unsecured claims. As noted earlier, Martin by mid-1987 had accumulated only $7.7 million in assets. In his May pre-sentencing memorandum the U.S. Attorney stated that an estimated $6.9 million in additional assets were "missing and concealed or unaccounted for." Given these circumstances, one could argue that C.H. had done alright for himself.

And C.H. in his plea bargaining had been able to do some things for other people. Charges of assisting in several of his schemes were dropped against his father, son Butch, and Butch's girl friend. Associate Gary Long received three years of probation, with a requirement that he give two speeches a year to civic groups on the values of American citizenship. Bank clerk Emma Bailey has similar citizenship responsibilities for three years of probation but only after she serves six months of a one-year prison sentence. Wife Shirley had her charges reduced to failure to report a crime and was given a three year sentence.

And David . . . Again

And then there was David Crabtree, always wheeling, dealing, moving money. When David headed off to prison in mid-1984, I observed that he might well receive his parole and be back in Knoxville and have no trouble identifying the old World's Fair site because it would likely be essentially the same.

As time moved on and we moved into the last quarter of 1986 the David Crabtree case reached the U.S. Office of Parole and David indeed was scheduled for parole in February 1987. A quick look at the site indicated that a social scientist might just be right in his prediction. But then . . . I had underestimated David.

In November 1986, the federal government indicted Crabtree, as part of the C.H. group, for concealing assets from the bankruptcy trustee of C.H., Jr., and wife Shirley. Under the terms of his 1984 plea agreement David supposedly was cooperating with the government as it put together its case against C.H. and others. But along the way David held back a little information. From his jail cell David, apparently thinking about the future, was moving, controlling some $1 million in U.S. Treasury notes and coupons--from C.H., Jr., through a friend to his (David's) wife.

"I screwed up bad," the 40-year old Crabtree told Judge Higgins as he pleaded guilty *(News-Sentinel,* March 13, 1987). Higgins agreed. On April 23, 1987, he sentenced Crabtree to five more years after he finished his earlier sentence, plus five additional years of probation. "David A. Crabtree," said Assistant U.S. Attorney Guy Blackwell in his pre-sentencing memorandum, "was, is and will always be a crook" *(Journal,* April 23, 1987).

Under such circumstances surely a social scientist shouldn't be held to a prediction. But no pity desired--yet. On the one hand, we shouldn't underestimate David again. On the other hand, site redevelopment has been anything but rapid. The old World's Fair site may still look all too familiar to the ultimate in deal makers when he is finally released.

CHAPTER 8

Cope and Hope

Compromised on the Way to the Fair

When the World's Fair ended in October 1982 hopes for redevelopment of its Lower Second Creek site were high. Indeed, talk of redevelopment had been prominent for years. At a July 1977 public hearing, John Ulmer, executive director of KCDC, the city's redevelopment agency, observed that construction would be under way "as soon as Expo moves out." Some were skeptical. "Try to be honest with the people," said Councilwoman Bernice O'Connor. But words kept coming. "We'll reach full potential in five years," said Ulmer.

And paper concerning redevelopment was not lacking. To see a city grant application to the federal government for more money for the World's Fair was to see a mini paper drive. Through the years, reported a *News-Sentinel* article of September 1984, the city had spent "close to $500,000 on fair planning and related activities, and site studies." Since that time, two more plans have emerged.

But talk and paper aside, fair site redevelopment had to overcome formidable obstacles. In particular, pre-fair decisions had greatly compromised the post-fair future.

With time pressures building, the $12.4 million U.S. Pavilion apparently could be designed and constructed with post-fair use in mind or it could be ready on time, but not both. The wedge-shaped six-story structure, said columnist Rex Reed of the New York *Daily News,* is "a pointless Tinker Toy" that "looks like Con Edison gone berserk." The pavilion was even more pointless than Rex was aware. It had no established post-fair use or user. But it had been ready for the fair on May 1, 1982.

Immediately to the south of the U.S. Pavilion and linking the main part of the valley site to the river front is a 16 acre tract of land along Second Creek and the Tennessee River. As noted in Book One, before the fair the property belonged to Southern Railroad and was scheduled to be acquired and used for the fair and afterward become part of the city's redevelopment project. But cost overruns played havoc with the plans, ultimately leaving the University of Tennessee with ownership after 1982. After spending $750,000 on improvements for the area the city government stood on the sidelines as a major component of the redevelopment site was turned into a UT surface parking lot with some of the best views and landscape architecture in the city.

Perhaps even more disruptive than the elimination of a linkage between the main site and the river is the Norfolk Southern railroad line to Alcoa, which runs through the middle of the site. "By any stretch of imagination a railroad is a blighting influence," said A.J. (Flash) Gray, a retired Tennessee Valley Authority planner who was hired by the city in 1980 to work on post-fair redevelopment. But meetings with railroad officials through the years seemed conclusive, Gray observed in a February 1985 interview. Removing the line would require a new bridge, estimated to cost $17 million, across the Tennessee River. "It might be that we would prefer, under certain conditions, leaving the railroad where it is," then city operations officer Bill Ricker said to the *News-Sentinel* back in February 1983.

But the situation got worse. After much heated discussion between city and railroad officials, Norfolk Southern in late 1985 erected a chain link fence on each side of the track out of concern for the safety of joggers and walkers and even parkers. In the process the elongated site was cut in half from one end to the other, with only one passageway left for pedestrian use. Norfolk Southern officials revealed, the *News-Sentinel* reported on November 21, 1985, that this was the arrangement agreed to by World's Fair officials during the land acquisition process, with KIEE establishing a $120,000 escrow fund for just that purpose. We're not the bad guys, Norfolk Southern officials told the *News-Sentinel*. We gave $2 million worth of property to the fair, and the 1982 agreement allows the city to build as many as three overpasses.

The verbal fallout continues. In a June 1987 interview, World's Fair site manager Jim Begalla stated that the city had carried a $10 million liability policy to cover possible mishaps. Well, I asked, why did they put up the fence? "Frankly, I don't know," he said. "I think they just wanted to spend the money." It was "just messing up their books."

Doesn't the railroad, Begalla was asked, need to be out of there, lock, stock and barrel? Although that would be great, it doesn't seem possible, Begalla said. The fair was run with the railroad there, he observed, "and we could too." But "we do need their cooperation. We need to be able to move across the site." And Begalla was hopeful. "I know they still have enough money in the account to take the fence down," he said.

As the above items illustrate, the prospects for immediate redevelopment of the site after the fair closed, optimistic statements notwithstanding, were not promising. Indeed, of the original 72 acre World's Fair site only some 21 acres remain available to the city for private development and much of this is characterized by steep slopes and sharp grade changes.

"The Fair site is not an easy site to develop," said Flash Gray in a *News-Sentinel* guest column of September 1984. And, as Gray already had discovered, the problems of redevelopment didn't involve site characteristics alone. The ugly face of politics was always there.

Victimized Again

By June 1981 Gray had produced a major study outlining a general re-use plan in the context of the limitations imposed by previous actions such as those mentioned above. Meanwhile, Mayor Tyree had established an advisory committee for the search and screening of a developer for the site. Additional studies, to the tune of $125,000, reported the *News-Sentinel* in January 1986, were conducted in 1982 by an Annapolis, Maryland, consulting firm that also assisted in finding a developer for the site.

"It was time to stop collecting paper," Gray later said in a February 1985 interview.

Following a national advertising campaign in 1982, four proposals for redevelopment were submitted, with Fairfield Communities' proposal for a combination of condominium and festive retail development being recommended to the mayor by the committee in early 1983.

"No politics was in it," said Gray. "I agreed with them." And the mayor "simply accepted the recommendation."

In its final form, Gray later wrote in the September 1984 guest column, the Fairfield plan "was a specific and concrete proposal to the city by a reputable, reliable and experienced developer to make an initial investment of $10 million on the site with the very likely prospect that this investment would be increased to over $50 million by the time the project was completed."

The plan didn't specifically deal with the U.S. Pavilion or with the southern part of the site or with commercial sites on the east. And because the plan called not only for a multi-phase development but also for one financed in part by $4.3 million of federal and city money, doubt still exists as to what Fairfield might have been or even if it would have been. (On November 3, 1985, in fact, former Mayor Tyree was quoted by the *News-Sentinel* as saying that a federal grant of $2 million "was not a for-sure situation" and the source of the city's other $2.3 million had not been decided.) But no doubt exists that, whatever Fairfield might have been was not to be, as the fair site was victimized again by the political forces at work in Knoxville, this time in the form of the mayoral election of 1983.

As the campaign unfolded the Fairfield plan became an issue between former Mayor Kyle Testerman (1972-1975), the presumed front-runner, who had been defeated eight years earlier by Tyree in 1975, and then Mayor Randy Tyree (1976-1983), who had chosen not to run for mayor in 1983, perhaps because of his dismal showing (22 percent) in Knox County as the Democratic candidate in the 1982 gubernatorial election. (In his 1982 run for the governor's office Tyree had depended heavily on Butcher bank loans to finance his campaign. He had been hurt locally when this fact was publicized during the campaign. He was hurt even more after the banks failed and repayment of the loans was sought by the FDIC. The presumption that Tyree would have run in 1983 had it looked right was given added weight when he announced as a candidate in the next election four years later.)

In any case, Tyree and the Fairfield developers apparently agreed on a development program in early 1983, but Tyree was a lame duck mayor who simply could not move city council. Time slipped by, and with time, opportunity.

Testerman took pains to point out in his campaign that he and his family had interests in apartment complexes in Knoxville, including one owned by his brothers in the Fort Sanders neighborhood adjacent to the fair site. But this, Testerman said, had nothing to do with his position, as he began to criticize the marketability of the condominium components of the Fairfield plan. When Testerman won the election, Fairfield saw the handwriting on the wall, cleared the board, and pulled out, reportedly already having dropped some $200,000-$300,000 in their Knoxville planning *(News-Sentinel,* January 31, 1986).

In interviews with the local newspapers in the aftermath of the election, Tyree and Testerman continued a sparring match that went back to 1975. It is a "political vendetta" against me, said Tyree. Fairfield knew better than to trust "a half-baked local politician" like Kyle. Redevelopment, Tyree said, is "back to square one."

Randy "can go his merry way," said Testerman. "It's a shame this site has been allowed to sit there for a year." His administration, Testerman said, would develop "a plan that will be exciting and provide this community protection for a fantastic development."

The Snails Take Over

Each of the pugilists had landed at least one decent blow. Redevelopment had returned to square one. And the site had been allowed to sit there for a year.

As his administration began in 1984, Testerman wasted little time in beginning the process of collecting more paper. He hired Harrison Price, a Los Angeles consulting firm, to conduct a feasibility study. In March 1984 Harrison Price presented preliminary findings.

It was as predictable as fleas on a dog. We had seen it half a dozen times or so. A few days before the consultant releases his study the two newspapers start to write front-page "insider-information" stories about the wonders to come. Puff it up. Then the study is released and the wonders-to-come are there. Sure enough, redevelopment is not only feasible, it's really feasible. The front pages are covered again. The city fathers exclaim, "Oh wonders," and "I just love the . . .," and "We can't wait." The newspapers editorialize, repeating the glow and "Let's get going."

And then the snails take over.

Harrison Price took a year to produce his final report, which was presented on March 5, 1985. Repeat Scene I. The details will have to be filled in by the selected developer, said Mayor Testerman.

The process began again to select a developer. "To keep politics out of the process" a non-profit body called Knoxville Tomorrow Incorporated (KTI), with 34 city fathers (29) and mothers (5) as members, was established on the heels of the Price report. By September 1985 KTI had worked out an arrangement with the city council whereby it would pick a developer and manage site development.

Six months before receiving its mandate from city council, KTI had started the process of selecting a master developer. At its very first meeting on March 15, 1985, it heard a presentation by Riverfronts Development Corporation of Columbia, Maryland. Riverfronts received an enthusiastic reception, and its spokesman, partner Robert Moon, was optimistic. If selected, the *News-Sentinel's* Roger Harris reported, Moon said work could begin by summer (but he didn't say what summer).

Three things about Riverfronts seemed to be particularly important. Two publicly known factors were that former CBS News anchorman Walter Cronkite was a partner in Riverfronts and that Mayor Testerman had already been in contact with Riverfronts. The unknown factor, which your author fell over quite by accident, was that Riverfronts was being represented in Tennessee by lawyer Lewis Donelson, a prominent west Tennessee Republican and former state commissioner of finance. In view of these three factors, even at an early stage in the game, Riverfronts seemed like a sure bet for selection as the site developer. But the process was not particularly rapid. Immediately after its formation in March 1985, Knoxville Tomorrow sent out inquiries to some 20 national firms. In addition to Riverfronts, only one other firm, Corley Capital Group of Washington, D.C., seemed to express serious interest. In January 1986, Mayor Testerman recommended and KTI selected Riverfronts of Knoxville, a spinoff from its parent Maryland firm, as the site's master developer. Everything thereafter would go through Riverfronts.

Riverfronts' basic plan was tourist and entertainment oriented with a festive retail area involving restaurants, nightclubs, and shops. A longer range picture saw potential for waterfront development to the south and a theme park to the north. It was quite a scheme. Included in the deal was $500,000 upfront city money for the developer to undertake pre-construction planning. The paper was getting more expensive.

By mid-November 1986, some 10 months later, a master plan had been developed by Riverfronts and approved by first KTI and then city council. Basically the plan is in line with Riverfronts' earlier indications, with the first phase of development being the festive retail Knoxville Place, to be located between the L&N Station and the Strohaus on property belonging to the Station '82 partnership. Under the approved plan, Riverfronts has nine months more to produce a detailed property acquisition, development, and financial plan for phase one, *including* how the city would be expected to participate. Riverfronts assured city council that it wouldn't take nine months. As recorded by the *News-Sentinel's* Roger Harris,

Riverfronts partner Jack Jones stated that he hoped "to have some activity on the fair site that people can enjoy in six to nine months."

As this manuscript nears completion, the eighth month is passing, and people are getting jumpy. Why the delays, the *Sentinel's* Andrew Oppmann asked Riverfronts' Robert Moon in mid-April 1987. "This is difficult work," responded Moon. And that indeed seems to be the case. Little is said publicly, but Riverfronts has not worked out property acquisition problems with Station '82. Developments regarding a next-door connector between Interstate 40 and downtown remain unsettled. And as will be seen below, other problems exist on the site as well.

"It's taken an agonizingly long time to get moving again," a *Journal* editorial observed on the occasion of the fifth anniversary of the opening of the fair. In an accompanying story reporter Tom Williams noted that yes, a developer exists, and yes, a master plan exists, "but so far, that plan is only on paper." Perhaps even more revealing, the *Journal* quoted Mayor Testerman as saying that perhaps we should leave the site as it is. "I'm personally pleased and happy with what's down there now."

Some Things Happened, But Not Much

The reader is no doubt aware that for the most part we left the fair site several pages back and wandered off into the realm of planning, of what might be. We can now, at least for a moment, return to the concrete "is." Just what has happened down there on the site since the gates closed on the 1982 World's Fair?

(The opportunity presents itself for your author to refer to the one time to his knowledge any element of the Knoxville media has referred in a positive way to his opposition to Expo '82. Get a little more, live a little better.)

"Joe was right, I suppose," wrote *Journal* columnist Jim Dykes on May 1, 1987. "When the gates swung shut, everything--and I mean everything!--went plumb to hell." Jim, as is his style, is exaggerating. But for that first year under the Tyree administration he was surely not far off base.

Original pre-fair plans called for KIEE to return the site to the city ready for the redevelopment phase. But KIEE simply didn't have any money for site clearance. As temporary structures were sold, dismantled, and hauled away, anything that wasn't of use to the buyers was left where it happened to fall. Especially visible was the four-acre pond, which saw its water level drop while litter accumulated. Vacant buildings attracted vagrants who "ripped off baseboards to heat themselves," observed Courtney Pearre, special counsel to the mayor. Inside and out, he said, "the site was in terrible condition" when the Testerman administration came into office in January 1984. The mayor, Pearre indicated in a December 1984 interview, was determined to clean the site and get people back into the area. And so he did.

With the use of the city's $1 million in federal Jobs Bill money, the site was cleaned, grass was sown, and the pond was cleaned and refilled. Site structures were restored to their condition at fair's end, and security was tightened. The site was dramatically changed.

Even while the cleanup was under way the city moved to bring activity to the site. In a September 1984 guest column in the *News-Sentinel* Mayor Testerman reported that 32 events had been held on the site during the previous five months. The events, said Lynn Polte of the city's public affairs office, ranged from a poorly attended bicycle race to the highly successful Riverfeast, a barbecue cooking contest that attracted an officially estimated 75,000 people over its two-day stand. And as we moved through 1985, 1986, and the first half of 1987, other events took place, occasionally large but mostly small. And the city has maintained the property, currently spending some $700,000 a year to do so, the *News-Sentinel* reported in April 1987. As compared with 1983 certainly, things were happening. But from the grand perspective of site development, not much. Indeed, the one potential project in the first half of Testerman's administration that looked like a for-real, right-now project of substantial consequence was vetoed by the mayor.

In May 1985 a proposal was made by Architectural Techniques (Artech) Corporation of Knoxville for an on-site $5.5 million, 240-unit condominium development. As carried by the local press on May 3, architect Jim Miller's description seemed impressive: two seven-story buildings connected by a glassed-in atrium, with an outdoor pool, and a 300-space parking garage, all designed to appeal to UT students and young professionals.

Of particular importance was the fact that the project was to occupy a small two-acre parcel of land cut off from the rest of the site by the Norfolk Southern line to the west, four-lane Main Avenue to the north, private apartment complexes to the south, and Poplar Street to the east.

"It seemed ideal to us," said Artech's Mike Brady in a June 1987 interview. The figures were right, he said, "and we had our financing all set." Artech was asking for no money from the city for parking garage or anything else. "All we wanted," said Brady, "was for the city to sell us the property at a reasonable price." And the project, Jim Miller had said earlier, would generate $120,000-$130,000 a year in taxes for the city.

Mayor Testerman shot down the proposal, just as he had earlier shot down that of Fairfield. In this case, however, his expressed opposition was based not on market conditions, but rather, according to the local press, on the project's incompatibility with the notion of a total site development plan and its restriction of access from the northern part of the site to the river.

Given the separated character of the property, neither argument seemed to make sense. So I called vice-Mayor and City Councilman Hoyle McNeil and asked about the project. The project just made sense, Hoyle said in June 1987. The papers favored it. The council favored it. "And I was really sold on the plan," he added. Everything seemed to be going well. Miller had several meetings with Testerman, Hoyle observed. But then "Kyle told him to forget it." Why? "Well, I don't know. Kyle probably had something else in mind." Probably.

One Positive, One Maybe

Without much question the most important positive concrete change on the site was the sale of the city-constructed office building to the state. The reader will remember this structure as part of the city's $21 million office-convention center complex. After use by the Expo Corporation during the fair, the office building was appraised at $5.5 million by the (Democrat) Tyree administration and then sat vacant until the (Republican) Testerman city administration was able to arrange a sale to the (Republican) Alexander state administration for $4.7 million.

"Did you take the city off the hook?" state architect Mike Fitts was asked in a June 1987 call to Nashville. "We're tighter than that," Fitts said. Pressed a bit, he said, "We thought it was in our interest." Back home in Knoxville, city official Courtney Pearre thought the same. The price is roughly equal to the building cost, he told a *News-Sentinel* reporter in July 1985. People, he said, were not "beating down the door to buy it."

As of mid-1987 the building was still unoccupied, but the state was nearing the end of a $1.4 million renovation, Fitts stated in that June telephone interview. But Mike, over in Nashville, hedged on an occupancy date. A call to the state elevator inspection office in Knoxville was a little better: "November supposedly, but maybe November of next year." The unknown responder continued, "Joe, you know how it goes with state government."

Do I? Well, sometimes the state government can take a heavy load off your shoulders. One load gone.

Potentially as important as the sale of the office building are the events that have occurred on the western part of the site in and around the seven restored Victorian houses and the Candy Factory, a four-story former warehouse that was renovated and occupied by restaurants during the fair.

As part of its clean-up efforts in 1983, the city moved to obtain occupants for the Victorian houses with the establishment of a mini artist colony that included shops on the ground level and living quarters above. Without question the local artists who leased them have struggled. But many have hung on, and things are getting better, site manager Jim Begalla said in a June 1987 interview. People are now breaking even, and as someone leaves, others come in, he continued. A walk through the area suggests that Jim surely is not understating the positives.

But something is there, and that something received a big boost when the old, and small, Dulin Gallery of Art changed its name to the Knoxville Museum of Art and moved into the Candy Factory in March 1987. Plans call for a future move in the summer of 1989 to a new 53,000 square foot, four-level museum building to be constructed next door. As of May 1987 the museum had raised $4.5 million of a needed $9.5 million for construction. The city had donated four acres of land and $1 million toward construction, with the state throwing in another $1 million.

And the ante for public expenditure may be raised. A campaign is under way for the development of an Art Park Group, including the Tennessee Amphitheater, the museum, the Candy Factory, and the artist colony. Group spokesperson (and also city official) Gloria Neel, reported the *News-Sentinel* at the end of May 1987, envisions a staff to schedule and promote events, with a budget derived from city leases of buildings in the area and other public sources.

No money comes in and more goes out. But . . . Art Park. A genuine public benefit may be developing.

Elsewhere, things look more shaky.

Opportunity Seems Everywhere

When Mayor Kyle Testerman came into office in January 1984, he began tossing off ideas like a dog shakes off water. To be sure, certain ideas seemed to be constants. He wanted something big, something different, something that would recapture the city's investment in the site, something that would attract tourists from the interstates. "We want a world class city," he wrote in the September 1984 guest column.

Not unlike others, including the planners, the mayor was thinking of everything: amusement, recreation, office, arts, food, retail, marina, Tivoli Gardens. He talked in terms of a multiplicity of uses for the U.S. Pavilion, ranging from a science museum to an atrium and convention center with a wrap-around hotel.

The mayor, observed *News-Sentinel* reporter Roger Harris at the end of Testerman's first year, is still exploring "a wide variety of ideas." As his fourth year nears an end, Testerman is still exploring, but frustration has been gaining. In mid-March 1987 he observed to the *News-Sentinel:* "The whole site's been one nightmare after another since the Fair quit." Six weeks later he was telling the *Journal* that maybe the site should be left as is. Another two weeks passed and he was telling everyone to tear down the U.S. Pavilion.

The basic problem in the redevelopment of the site is that nothing jumps out at you, or perhaps better stated, too many things jump out at you, and all cost money.

The site is indeed an attractive one. And it already has, exclusive of land acquisition and site improvements, some $70 million (better than $50 million of which is public money) in developments.

Surely something must be possible, the observer thinks, as he stands on the northern hill that once featured the fair's folklife festival. Below, stretching down the valley, are a multiplicity of improvements: the renovated L&N Station; the convention center; the hotel; the (now) state office building; the Sunsphere; the U.S. Pavilion; the Tennessee Amphitheater; the Candy Factory; the Victorian houses; the nine acre pond and surrounding park land; and the additional 21 acres of grassed open space.

Opportunity seems everywhere. But most have limitations, even dilemmas, associated with them.

The site has a new convention center. But in terms of cost, location, and design the convention center stands out as one of the worst decisions of the Expo promoters. If we take the office building sale price of $4.7 million off the original $21 million combined cost of the two buildings, the convention center's cost is $16.3 million, without a doubt well over the cost of comparable facilities. And with regard to industry standards, the convention center building is simply inadequate, which is not surprising in view of the fact that little if anything in the way of a feasibility study was undertaken. In any case, the center has poor acoustics (supposedly currently being corrected), poor exhibit access, and, at 77,349 square feet, is too small, says Mayor Testerman and others. Gloria Neel, the city's director of housing and urban affairs, raised the possibility of a new larger facility in the downtown area. (Should a new facility be constructed, the city would then have its old and newly renovated civic auditorium/coliseum complex east of the downtown area; its "new-new" convention center a half-mile west in the center of downtown; and its "old-new" convention center another half mile west on the World's Fair site. And then one mile further west on the UT campus, there is the new 25,000 seat UT arena/assembly center, currently being built in large part with local government funds and supposedly available for large public occasions such as conventions. Some might say that if this is planning, perhaps we should forget planning and just go back to doing things.)

The imposing U.S. Pavilion, constructed at a cost of $12.4 million, is perhaps *the* albatross of site redevelopment. The pavilion's pre-fair history was explored in Book One. After the fair the General Services Administration (GSA), the federal agency with the responsibility of disposing of surplus property, first sought federal government users for the pavilion. No takers. Then it advertised for bids from the general public. No bids. [Salt is rubbed in the taxpayers' wound. While all this was happening, the U.S. government was planning and ultimately was constructing a new $12 million, six-story federal office building three blocks from the location of the federal pavilion.]

Aside from the 1982 World's Fair, perhaps no other event or thing in the city's history has received more newspaper ink. Weekly it seems, a new user and use presents itself, glows on page one for a time and then quietly fades while the next user presents the next use. As this manuscript approaches send-off time, Digital A.V., a local "high-tech" firm, has been in the glow for several weeks, perhaps taking more time to fade because this all-but-certain user was announced by none other than Riverfronts partner Walter Cronkite. The stumbling block now, as in the past, is conversion cost estimates, said to be some $3 million this time around, although costs in the past have ranged from $6-8 million. Recent news accounts from Digital have been either all positive with a slight negative or all negative with a slight positive. Who knows?

In the meantime, Mayor Testerman is saying on the one hand that the pavilion should be torn down, and on the other hand that it should be bought by the city for GSA's $1.1 million price tag. Perhaps the two hands will come together. [Dateline--last minute. History repeated itself. Digital A.V. quietly faded. GSA will auction off the building on September 29, 1987.]

As the reader may recall from Book One, three major private structures on the site--the Holiday Inn parking garage, the Sunsphere, and the L&N Station--received "loans" before the fair collectively totaling over $12 million, for which they were to make interest-only payments, again collectively, of $700,000 a year to the city. In addition, lease payments of $200,000 were to be made by the Holiday Inn for 29,000 square feet of convention center space housing the hotel's lobby, bar, and swimming pool. The total of $900,000 a year was to go toward the city's $1.9 million payments for retiring its $21 million debt on the convention center/office building.

All of these projects have experienced serious economic problems. The most serious has been the Sunsphere, the theme structure of the fair. As soon as the fair was over, the Sunsphere's restaurant hit hard times, ultimately pulling out in March 1984, having lost $1 million in the past year, the mayor told the *News-Sentinel*. As the owners tottered on the brink of foreclosure regarding a private loan, the city passed a bond issue of over $1.4 million in December 1986 and purchased the building. Instead of receiving $130,000 yearly for 30 years, the Sunsphere's share of that $900,000, the city will now be paying out an average of over $190,000 a year for the next 15 years to retire a new debt. No cost? No risk? Perhaps a good luck spell could be generated with a new name. Let's call it the Sunspot.

(Interestingly enough, on the same day that city council was passing the bond issue, a group of parents in Knoxville's eastside black community was threatening a boycott of Vine Middle School. The school, Reverend W. C.

Parker of Peace and Goodwill Missionary Baptist Church told the *News-Sentinel's* Marti Levary, is falling in and is a fire trap already declared hazardous by state fire inspectors. Newspaper pictures backed up the charges.)

But the story doesn't stop here. In order to get something in the Sunspot the city signed a five-year lease with the Arts Council, a local non-profit arts promotion group, for $1 a year, with the city paying utilities. Ultimately, planners say, the Sunspot may become a night-club. Should this ever occur, expectations are that it would be turned over to the operator at a reduced or perhaps no cost.

The new 299-room Holiday Inn also has experienced major financial problems, with its owner currently on the brink of default. At this writing the bond insurer was paying the interest on the bonds, and owner Franklin Haney was trying to sell the hotel and its attached 450-space parking garage. Initially Haney made loan payments (theoretically $575,000 a year for the hotel and the garage) as well as tax payments to the city, but he is now well behind in both. In mid-June 1987 the *News-Sentinel* reported that the hotel had lost $1.6 million last year.

Mayor Testerman has acknowledged that the hotel's payments to the city will have to be cut in order to make the hotel viable. Yet as of mid-June he was unable to work out an arrangement with the only known serious potential buyer for the hotel. In dropping his purchase offer, Mark Oldham of Nashville's U.S. Hospitality Corporation told the *News-Sentinel's* Jack Lail: "Apparently he doesn't want to work with me. . . . He wants to work with someone else." No "someone else" has been mentioned to date.

The picture for the Holiday Inn as well as for other hotels in the downtown area has been marred by slow recovery in the hotel occupancy rate after the 1982 fair. In the central business district, for example, Pannell Kerr Forster's statistical review of occupancy rates showed a 64 percent rate in 1980, dropping off to 55 percent in 1981, as new hotels came into operation, and then increasing to 71 percent in 1982. The 1983 data reveal a depression in the downtown hotel industry with a post-fair dropoff to 44 percent. Since that time the figure has come in at around 55 percent in 1984, 1985, and 1986. The first quarter of 1987 showed a 49 percent rate, thereby signifying that no dramatic improvement is likely in 1987. It's been "real rough," former Hyatt Regency general manager Paul Sherbakoff told the *News-Sentinel* in May 1987.

Outwardly the L&N Station, with three restaurants, an art gallery, and leased office space in tow, seems quite viable as an economic operation. Yet it too has experienced cash-flow difficulties, partly because of its $195,000 yearly obligation to the city and partly because of its private loans now held by the FDIC in the wake of the Butchers' bank failures. In early 1985 the L&N went into voluntary bankruptcy in order to secure protection from its creditors. In mid-February 1987 owner Alex Harkness told the *News-Sentinel* that he had emerged from bankruptcy proceedings after successfully reorganizing his finances.

Uplift Politics

Positive things have occurred on the site. And opportunities seemingly are unlimited. But everywhere one sees problems. Getting off dead center, even as we approach the fifth anniversary of the closing of the fair, is still not easy.

Perhaps we should begin by placing the site and site redevelopment in perspective. Cycles of runaway expectations followed by images of failure may be not only irrational but also self-defeating. Knoxville's civic leaders may need to recall that when geographer Robert Pierce concluded in 1984 that Knoxville was one of the two most livable cities in the United States, he was using pre-fair data. The World's Fair site, Bill Sansom, then president of the local Chamber of Commerce and formerly the state financial commissioner, told the *News-Sentinel* a few years back, is an asset that needs "to get hitched up and running." But, he added, and more importantly, it is not something that will "make or break Knoxville."

Our focus on the fair site may be harming our overall performance. "The city needs more people living in center city" is a truism accepted by many, most, perhaps all of the groups and individuals concerned with Knoxville's redevelopment process; but when they think of where, the answer is usually the fair site or the downtown area. Does anyone talk about inner-city neighborhood revitalization anymore?

Knoxville also needs to recognize that, without question, additional public money will be needed, whatever might be done with the site. Redevelopment of the site is now and always has been a risky business. That's why the city has had so few possible takers in several major national sales efforts. Public officials should face this fact and let the people who pay the bills in on the secret. What the fair was supposed to produce will have to be paid for anew. Whether the World's Fair was good or bad, the people who sold it fed us a substantial pile of *(Watership Down)* "hraka."

The time may be approaching when the city should stop thinking in terms of a grand slam or nothing. Even if Riverfronts, the current master developer, stays on the scene, the pace of development is unlikely to be rapid. Perhaps even more important, the script will change frequently as the years pass. The city should acknowledge these facts and let the potential innovators, the entrepreneurs, know it. And when a legitimate developer with a legitimate proposal and real money comes along, give him the ball, even if he's not a brother or a party-mate or a whatever.

In order to make wise political decisions, with or without Riverfronts, relative to the site or elsewhere, politics in Knoxville needs to be uplifted. With the power of Jake Butcher behind the scenes, Knoxville for several years was able to make big decisions, a number of which have created s rious problems for the city's future. Decision-making has now become a more difficult task. But let us recognize that decision-making in an open society is not supposed to be easy. Indeed, our suspicions should be aroused when things look too smooth. The city, however, needs more than simply the ability to work out its hard decisions. It also needs a different quality to its decisions. Knoxville of all places is unlikely to see the politics taken out of politics. Perhaps, however, it can get some public interest into politics. We are surely a long way from the political picture of Knoxville in the 1920s that was described by Louis Brownlow back in chapter 3. We need to get further.

But I digress. It's the redevelopment of the World's Fair site that we're dealing with here, and as we depart the site, its future seems cloudy. It is not exactly empty, but surely it is far too empty. Without question, however, the site is not dead, will not die. And no doubt it will be used more frequently for more events by more people. But relative to the grand design, no one can say what the site will look like five or ten years from now.

Indeed, the *Journal's* Tom Williams writes (May 1, 1987) that even Riverfronts' Robert Moon says it's hard for him to visualize what the site will be. Citing his experience with Baltimore's Inner Harbor, Moon says (if not exactly this way) that you do something, and you gain momentum, and then other things follow, and then when it's there, you know what it is.

So there we have it: cope and hope.

CHAPTER 9
Will They Get It?

"COURAGE, READER! WE NEAR THE END," said Will Durant as he concluded volume six of *The Story of Civilization*. Ten years, four volumes, and 3,523 pages later, Durant finally reached the end. Most fortunately, the courage of the current reader (and writer) will not be so tested, as we approach a more imminent end to one observer's view of Knoxville and aspects of its political life from early 1982 to the summer of 1987.

Knoxville did have its fair in 1982. And in a number of respects the World's Fair in and of itself was reasonably successful. Indeed, for some it was a golden event. But for many others, World's Fair oversell was not an abstraction.

Nor was the post-fair period a mere abstraction for Jake and C.H. Butcher, Jr. The fair at least in part was linked to their personal collapse as well as the failure of their banking empires. But the story of the Butchers began long before the fair with personal behavior and banking practices that led to their downfall regarding not only their financial status and political power but also their personal freedom.

And then we have the whole notion of broader social fallout from the fair, including redevelopment of the site itself. The promoters were strong on promises, but weak on performance. And the city has been left with too few benefits and too many costs. Whatever else it might have been, the 1982 World's Fair was no bargain for the public.

As we look back over the topics covered in Book Two, is there a set of themes, an ordering perspective that presents itself? And relatedly, we may ask: are the political activities to which we have been exposed unique to our city? Was the Butcher crowd and its modes of operation truly exotic in contemporary American society?

Evidence from the national economic and political scene suggests that, for all the particular differences, the Knoxville case was not unique. Indeed, as we move through the 1980's we increasingly hear of a society characterized by deceit and hypocrisy and unethical self-serving behavior, with self-indulgence at the public trough increasingly a part of the American way of life.

Using FBI data on closed cases, the "Corporate Crime Reporter," a weekly newsletter on white-collar crime, said that fraud and embezzlement had led to record U.S. bank losses of $1.1 billion in 1986, up more than 30 percent over the losses of 1985 *(News-Sentinel,* July 20, 1987). But the money-crazed bankers don't stand alone. In late 1985 the Associated Press carried a major article on corporate crime in which prominent sociologist Amitai Etzioni of George Washington University is cited as stating that more is involved than a few rotten apples. "We should stop looking at the apples and look at the barrel," said Etzioni, whose research finds dramatic levels of illegal activities among our business leaders *(Knoxville Journal,* December 25, 1985).

And, said the *New York Times'* Winston Williams (June 9, 1985), you don't have trouble identifying the players, as he ticked off "such once-venerable names as General Dynamics, General Electric, E.F. Hutton, E.M.S. Securities, and Bank of Boston." Corporate morality, said Williams, is being eroded by "economic pressures, a new permissiveness and simple greed." It isn't surprising that our own Jake Butcher made Williams' article on "mushrooming corporate crime."

Jake again made the list when *Time* magazine gave unethical behavior top billing on May 25, 1987, and extended the discussion into the broad sweep of American society. *Time's* 20-page set of articles ran a cover description that asked "What Ever Happened to Ethics." Focusing only on recent revelations, *Time* pointed to where it's located: Wall Street financiers, presidential candidates, Washington lobbyists, television evangelists, the U.S. Marines, the inner core of the White House. And to actions ranging "from weakness of will to moral laxity to hypocrisy to uncontrolled avarice." America, said *Time,* is "wallowing in a moral morass."

Not surprisingly, these views are compatible with those right here at home. *Washington Post* writer David Broder came down to Knoxville, talked to the locals, had a national and a local opinion survey taken and concluded that Knoxville, like elsewhere in the country, had a "sour climate." People, Broder said, are looking for honesty and integrity in government but they "tell you they are convinced they won't get it" *(Asheville Citizen,* April 22, 1987). (The broader "A Grass-Roots Report: Voters Voice Increasing Disillusionment," appeared in the *Washington Post,* April 22, 1987.)

This is not a pretty picture, either locally or nationally. And the closer one looks at it the easier it is to identify with Clare Boothe Luce when she said: "I tend to be a pessimist because a lifetime of experience has convinced me that the difference between an optimist and a pessimist is that the pessimist is better informed."

But what the country needs is not informed pessimists but informed optimists, people who know the system and are willing to work to obtain reform. As can be seen in the present study, however, efforts to bring about change frequently reap experiences analogous to that of boxer James (Quick) Tillis on his first day in Chicago. As reported in *Sports Illustrated*, Quick put down his suitcase, looked up at the Sears Tower and said, "Chicago, I'm going to conquer you." When he looked down his suitcase was gone.

Granted, many suitcases will be lifted, but change can be made in the system, faults can be conquered. Reformers should take their motto from Edmund Burke who long ago said: "The only thing necessary for the triumph of evil is for good men to do nothing."